Aspects of modern sociology

SOCIAL PROCESSES

GENERAL EDITORS

John Barron Mays

Emeritus Professor of Sociology, University of Liverpool

Maurice Craft

Professor of Education, University of Nottingham

ASPECTS OF MODERN SOCIOLOGY

General Editors

John Mays Emeritus Professor of Sociology, University of Liverpool
Maurice Craft Professor of Education, University of Nottingham

This Longman library of texts in modern sociology consists of three Series, and includes the following titles:

THE SOCIAL STRUCTURE OF MODERN BRITAIN

The family
Mary Farmer
formerly University of Liverpool

The political structure
Grace Jones
Chester College of Higher Education

Population
Prof. R. K. Kelsall
formerly University of Sheffield

Education
Ronald King
University of Exeter

The welfare state
Prof. David Marsh
formerly University of Nottingham

Crime and its treatment
Prof. John Barron Mays
University of Liverpool

Structures and processes of Urban life
Prof. R. E. Pahl
University of Kent
R. Flynn
University of Salford
N. H. Buck
University of Kent

The working class
Kenneth Roberts
University of Liverpool

The middle class
Prof. John Raynor
The Open University
and
Roger King
Huddersfield Polytechnic

Leisure
Kenneth Roberts
University of Liverpool

The mass media
Peter Golding
University of Leicester

Mental illness
Bernard Ineichen
University of Bristol

The economic structure
Prof. Cedric Sandford
University of Bath

SOCIAL PROCESSES

Communication
Prof. Denis McQuail
University of Amsterdam

Stratification
Prof. R. K. Kelsall
formerly University of Sheffield
H. Kelsall
formerly Doncaster College of Education
L. Chisholm
University of Maryland, Heidelberg

Socialisation
Graham White
University of Liverpool

Social conflict
Prof. John Rex
University of Aston

Forthcoming titles will include:

Migration
Prof. J. A. Jackson
University of Dublin

SOCIAL RESEARCH

The limitations of social research
Prof. M. D. Shipman
University of Warwick

The philosophy of social research
John Hughes
University of Lancaster

Data collection in context
Stephen Ackroyd
and
John Hughes
University of Lancaster

BY HELEN AND KEITH KELSALL

Social Disadvantage and Educational Opportunity (1971)
The School Teacher in England and the United States (1969)

BY KEITH KELSALL

Population (4th edn 1979)
Graduates: the Sociology of an Elite (with A. Poole and A. Kuhn) (1972)
Six Years After (with A. Poole and A. Kuhn) (1970)
Women and Teaching (1963)
Applications for University Admission (1957)
Higher Civil Servants in Britain (1955)
Wage Regulation under the Statute of Artificers (1938, repub. 1972)

Stratification

An Essay on Class and Inequality

Second edition

Keith Kelsall

Emeritus Professor of Sociology University of Sheffield

Helen M. Kelsall

Formerly Senior Lecturer in Education
Doncaster College of Education

Lynne Chisholm

Lecturer
University of Maryland, Heidelberg

Longman
London and New York

Longman Group Limited
Longman House, Burnt Mill, Harlow
Essex CM20 2JE, England
Associated companies throughout the world

Published in the United States of America
by Longman Inc., New York

First published 1974, 1984

British Library Cataloguing in Publication Data
Kelsall, R. Keith
Stratification: an essay on class and inequality.
—2nd ed.—(Aspects of modern sociology. Social processes)
1. Equality
I. Title II. Kelsall, Helen M.
III. Chisholm, Lynne IV. Series
305 HM146

ISBN 0-582-29563-7

Library of Congress Cataloguing in Publication Data

Kelsall, Roger Keith, 1910–
Stratification: an essay on class and inequality.
(Aspects of modern sociology. Social processes)
Bibliography: p.
Includes index.
1. Social classes. 2. Equality. 3. Social mobility.
I. Kelsall, Helen M. II. Chisholm, Lynne. III. Title.
IV. Series.
HT609.K38 1984 305.5'12 83-18797
ISBN 0-582-29563-7

Printed in Singapore by Selector Printing Co

Contents

Editors' Preface	viii
Foreword	ix
Part One: Avowed inequality—three examples	
1 Slave, caste and feudal relationships	3
Part Two: Avowed equality yet widespread inequality: Britain and the United States	
2 Introduction	15
3 Differing theoretical orientations	18
4 Economic inequality	25
5 Power inequality in community and society	34
6 Power inequality within sectors and occupations	49
7 Status inequality	61
8 How many dimensions, and how are they interrelated?	71
9 Inequality of life expectancy	76
10 Inequality of access to educational and career opportunities	82
11 Inequality of access to housing	89
12 Class-related attitudes and behaviours	94
13 Differing constructions of reality	103
14 Social mobility	114
15 Sexual stratification and social stratification	134
16 Themes of current debate	146
Postscript on state socialist societies	158
References and further reading	164
Index of names	
Index of subjects	

Editors' Preface

The first series in Longman's *Aspects of Modern Sociology* library was concerned with the social structure of modern Britain, and was intended for students following professional and other courses in universities, polytechnics, colleges of education, and elsewhere in further and higher education, as well as for those members of a wider public wishing to pursue an interest in the nature and structure of British society.

A further series set out to examine the history, aims, techniques and limitations of social research; and this third series is concerned with a number of fundamental social processes. The presentation in each case is basically analytical, but each title will also seek to embody a particular viewpoint. It is hoped that these very relevant introductory texts will also prove to be of interest to a wider, lay readership as well as to students in higher education.

JOHN BARRON MAYS
MAURICE CRAFT

Foreword

This book is about inequality, or more specifically, social inequality. In explaining what we mean by this we can take as our yardstick adult males in the prime of life and their families. Then what we are concerned with is the extent to which they appear to be, or to have been, unequally treated in the society in which they live and work[1].

One major area of interest concerns the *respects* in which they are or have been unequally treated. Perhaps the most basic respect is that of their legal and political rights. We have become so accustomed to assuming that nominal equality before the law and manhood suffrage are basic social principles, that we tend to forget that they are not in fact cultural universals and that alternative approaches have frequently been found. In Europe in the later Middle Ages, for example, members of the different 'estates' often had varying legal rights and duties, and there could be discrepancies between the penalties laid down for the same offence. These were sometimes of an unexpected kind, as when on the basis of *noblesse oblige* there were heavier penalties for members of the nobility than for others.

A second obvious respect in which people fare differently relates to their economic position. Incomes tend to be very unequal: wealth is unevenly distributed. The possible reasons for such inequalities, whether we view the matter from an individual or from a societal level, are, as we shall see later, very complex. Again, these differences in incomes and in wealth are clearly partly, but not wholly, responsible for differences in life styles. They equally obviously tend to be associated with differences in economic power, though not in an entirely straightforward manner. Moreover, a picture of the members of any society in terms of the distribution of economic power would not in any case necessarily be identical with that showing the distribution of, say, political power or military power.

So when we speak of social inequality we include such matters as legal and political rights, economic resources either of an income or of a capital kind, and power of all types. And even this does not exhaust the subject, for the scope of such a term has to be wide enough also to include inequalities in status, that is in social honour or prestige.

Perhaps it will be clearer with what kinds of inequality we are *not* concerned if we note that the types we have mentioned so far have, or are intended to have, one thing in common, namely that they are *structured* inequalities which appear to be closely linked with the institutional arrangements in a given society. They are not fortuitous, but whether intentionally or otherwise, they form what is virtually a built-in feature of the social system. The distinction between these and other respects in which people can be seen to be unequal is a very difficult one to make, though we have to try and make it.

From what has been said it will be clear that the matters with which we are concerned relate not to all types of social differentiation but only to differentiation involving inequality. In other words, when we look at how adult males and their families have fared in a particular society in any one of the respects we have outlined, there begins to emerge a pattern not just of differences but of inequalities. The outcome has to have been unequal in the sense that we (and they) could use such terms as 'superior' or 'inferior', 'better' or 'worse' (and also give some indication of degree), to describe how they had fared relatively to each other. It is, of course, also essential that the inequalities being studied should relate to things that are socially valued, where a large measure of consensus regarding the desirability of having more rather than less can be taken for granted.

At this point a practical difficulty arises. We can hardly hope to discuss in any useful way the almost infinite degrees of inequality in any given respect of all the adult males and their families in a particular society. Instead, it becomes necessary to deal in terms of groups of people similarly situated in the respect being considered, so that what we are describing and attempting to explain becomes in effect a series of layers or strata. There are obvious objections to this type of simplification. In the first place, how can we be sure that the grouping we are using is a satisfactory one? Are the differences, for example, between adjacent groups greater or in some other way more significant than the differences within the groups? A second and related objection arises from the use of the term stratum with its geological associations, for this seems to imply both a degree of permanence which may or may not be justified, and also to imply that there is some very basic difference between adjacent strata of a kind which is entirely distinct from any variations within the strata themselves, and this too may or may not be misleading. Nevertheless, the term *social stratification* has become the conventional one to use, and we have to make the best of it.

It has already been made clear that the profiles of social inequality in terms of each of the different types of such inequality may not be identical with each other. That is to say, some individuals and families will fare better relatively to the rest on one dimension of inequality compared with another. The crucial question to which we shall have to return later is whether these incongruities are so important as altogether to invalidate the concept of social groupings who fare well or badly in *all* or most respects. For the moment we must leave this issue on one side.

However misleading in certain respects the term may be, then, social stratification, in the sense described, is what this book is about. And the aspects of it with which we shall be concerned include, first, the apparent link between particular features of the social stratification pattern and specific basic characteristics of certain societies. Secondly, in the case of societies of the type of Britain and the United States we plan to look fairly closely at what appear to be the factors accounting for different types of inequality, and also what appear to be the main consequences of these inequalities. And in the course of this some indication is likely to emerge as to which of various alternative theories, models and concepts is apparently most useful in contributing to an understanding of what takes place. The whole subject, moreover, becomes even more complicated when we realise that different people may have different conceptions of what the social inequalities in the communities in which they live and work actually are, different views as to the legitimacy or otherwise of what they see, and different reactions to what they see in the sense of how they behave and encourage others to behave. We propose to discuss, then (*a*) the extent and nature of these inequalities, (*b*) why they exist, and (*c*) why they seem (if in fact they do) to be so persistent. We shall be concerned with stratification as a *social process* and we shall treat inequality not just as an attribute of individuals or families but as involving *social relationships* of various kinds (for example, between employer and worker, landlord and tenant, or between two people, one of whom receives and the other accords, deference in their social interaction).

One very important point to which attention must be drawn at the outset is that our concern is with the situation of a person or a group *relative* to that of another person or group. We are not considering how someone's position has improved or deteriorated in an *absolute* sense. An economist might point out, for instance, that the welfare of the poor is better served by concentrating attention on the growth rate rather than on the distribution of the national income. And some kinds and degrees of social inequality may to an unknown extent in certain types of society be a prerequisite for economic growth, so that trying to reduce these disparities may be killing the goose that lays the golden egg. While in quite a different context, the interests of poor people with very young babies might lie rather in advancing medical knowledge leading to an overall decline in the infant mortality rate than in knowing more about why a social class *differential* in the propensity to die before one's first birthday exists. All this is perfectly true, and we can only plead that problems of structured social inequality are nevertheless important enough to justify devoting a book to them, whilst not denying that across-the-board improvements in social welfare generally are just as desirable and worthy of study.

And it is as well to make our position in regard to value judgements explicit rather than leaving it merely implicit. We are against structured social inequality of all kinds, and the reader should know this in order to make allowance for it, since our approach and our evaluation of other people's work may well have been coloured by this circumstance.

When a revised edition of this book was needed, to take account of the considerable volume of relevant new published work appearing between the mid-1970s and the mid-1980s, the original authors sought the help of Lynne Chisholm, with whom they had worked before and whose interests made her a particularly appropriate collaborator. Whilst all three of us share responsibility for the revised edition as a whole, she did the bulk of the necessary re-writing of chapters 4 (Economic inequality), 14 (Social mobility), and 16 (Themes of current debate), besides writing an important and entirely new chapter (15) on Sexual stratification and social stratification.

PART ONE
Avowed inequality—three examples

Slave, caste and feudal relationships 1

From our point of view one of the most fundamental distinctions to be made at the outset is between societies in which there is supposed to be basic equality of treatment as between all adult males and their families, and societies in which avowedly, openly and deliberately there is *inequality* of treatment at least in certain vital matters. Contemporary Britain and the United States of America can be taken as examples of the first type of situation, and the main part of the present book will consist of discussion of illustrative material from these two societies. Before embarking on this, however, we plan to look at three situations coming into the second of these categories. The cases we propose briefly to discuss involve societies in which, amongst many other features distinguishing them from each other, there is one particular characteristic on which attention will be focused, namely the existence within them of a specific type of social relationship involving open, avowed and deliberate inequality between specified groups of people.

SLAVE RELATIONSHIPS

The common characteristic of all societies which contain some adults correctly describable as slaves is that these people are distinguished from all other adults by having virtually no legal rights, and by being in effect the chattels of their masters.[1] Having said this much, however, we are immediately faced with a whole variety of respects in which the position in any given society is not likely to be as clearcut as this simple statement might lead us to suppose. Are the slaves distinguished by some racial or ethnic feature from the rest of the community? Has their situation resulted from conquest, or have they sometimes fallen into slavery through becoming debtors? Is the master's power over them absolute, and if not, what are the restrictions legal and other on it? Do unions between male and female slaves take the form of marriage? Do those whose mothers/fathers were slaves automatically have the same ascription? Can slaves acquire or inherit any form of property, personal or otherwise, or enter into any type of contract? In what circumstances is manumission possible, and how frequently does this take place?

We would not expect that the answers to these and many other questions would necessarily be the same in every society where some slaves were present. For though the slave is universally a chattel he is also a living chattel and a human being, and there may be certain human rights however rudimentary that the society in which he lives allows him. Some writers have stressed the extent to which the legal situation of slaves was similar in such diverse settings as ancient Greece and Rome on the one hand and America before the civil war on the other. Perhaps all this shows is that once you have adults who are denied many of the rights that even the worst situated free man possesses, there is likely to follow in practice a whole set of other derivative characteristics affecting a wide range of legal and quasilegal matters.

For our purposes it is probably sufficient to bypass the many complexities of the slave situation and to regard it merely as an extreme form of legal inequality with far-reaching political, economic and social consequences both for the individual and for society. Slavery has often, perhaps usually, been a means to an end so far as the master was concerned, the end being that of getting work done and tasks performed. Forced labour is, then, a necessary part of the slave situation, but not all forced labour is to be regarded as slavery. For example, the family of a man subject to forced labour may not so be involved, his descendants may not be forced to work as he is, his plight may be for a limited period, he may retain some legal rights pertaining to a free man other than those directly concerned with his work.

It hardly needs to be emphasised that the disappearance of slavery was often associated with a growing realisation by the masters (or by employers in general) of the relative inefficiency and expensiveness of this way of getting work done, and also with the increasing difficulty of reconciling such an arrangement with types of religious belief (where these were prevalent) in which stress was laid on the equality of all human beings in the eyes of God.

CASTE RELATIONSHIPS

It is well known that the Hindu areas of India have traditionally been characterised by very detailed and complicated sets of social rules governing the day-to-day relations of the village inhabitants with each other, the community being divided into hereditary groups known as castes. The details vary from one quite small area to another and have been modified in course of time, but certain underlying common principles are readily discernible which can be taken as characteristic of the Hindu Indian caste system as an ideal type. The groups can be seen to form a status hierarchy, the rules are clearly designed to ensure their separation from each other, but in the accompanying division of labour their interdependence as well as their separateness is manifest. The basic principle underlying the whole caste system is the opposition of the pure and the impure. Thus the hierarchical element derives from the superiority of the pure to the impure; if the pure is not to be polluted by the impure, separation is vital. An initial division of labour is likewise centred on the need to keep separate pure and impure occupations and those who are engaged in them. It can readily be seen, therefore, that what we are concerned with is a system of ideas and values, and that the values in this case are religious ones. It is no accident that the Brahmins or priests form the apex of the structure. Between them and the lowest caste (sometimes referred to as the 'Untouchables') people are classified on the basis of degrees of dignity and fastidiousness, but the ranking of itself does not tell us anything directly about the distribution of power.

The practical implementation of the pure/impure principle by which the separateness of the castes is maintained includes detailed arrangements for the prevention or containment of impurity by laying down from whom one can receive drinking water, what kind of food can be eaten, and by whom and in what ways it should be prepared. It also encompasses all social relationships, from eating, walking or working with others to such questions as marriage and where one can live. Though information on what actually happens or is permissible in hypothetical circumstances naturally varies somewhat according to the informant, at least those responsible for an Indian population census (e.g. that of 1901) could, on the basis of finding out what kind of meat one ate, what one's attitude was on the remarriage of widows and so on, provide an approximation to classifying people in caste terms. How different, not only in degree but in kind, has been the task faced by the Registrar General for England and Wales in a totally different type of society when seeking to subdivide the population into social class groups. To Western eyes, of course, many of the practices laid down by the caste rules appear either ludicrous (as with the Brahmins' frequent baths or throwing away of food contaminated by the shadow of an 'Untouchable') or barbarous. But a study of the social refinements found to be operating in certain sections of English society can equally easily form the subject of ridicule.[2]

We must not, of course, exaggerate the rigidity of the caste system whose basic features we have been trying to indicate. Movement across caste barriers intergenerationally or intragenerationally is not completely ruled out, and certainly takes place in the case of individuals, families and sometimes whole groupings. Though social mobility is naturally less likely to occur than in an individualistic society it is not by any means precluded. As illustrating this, while members of each caste (or more correctly each subcaste) are at pains to protect themselves and their children against demotion by limiting the choice of marriage partners to their own group, in the second and subsequent marriage of women there is a good deal more flexibility. It is equally an exaggeration to suppose that by being born into a particular caste, men can in adult life only follow a specified profession or occupation. Provided a way of earning one's living is not markedly less pure than that traditional to the caste no harm is done; and an increasing number of occupations have come to be regarded as neutral in terms of the pure/impure dichotomy.

The types of inequality inherent in the caste system, with its religious orientation and emphasis on status, do not, as we have said, *directly* bear on inequalities of economic and political power. To bring in this power element we have to make reference to the classical theory of the varnas, intended to apply throughout India, where a hierarchy of four varnas or estates, differing from that deriving from the pure and impure, is found. This is a hierarchy of function rather than of birth and also involves differential privileges and differential legal situations for the estates concerned, which comprise first the Brahmins (priests), then the Kshatriyas (warriors or kings), the Vaishyas (farmers or merchants) and the Shudras (servants or have-nots), with the 'Untouchables' falling outside the classification. The coexistence of the caste system and the theory of the varnas presents obvious difficulties. For example, how can a king who eats meat be more highly regarded than a farmer who is a vegetarian? For our purposes, however, it seems sufficient to stress at this point the vital importance of the distinction made between priesthood and royalty, the separation of status and power and therefore of spiritual authority and temporal authority, the king having no religious prerogatives.

If we examine the matter at the village level we find that the land is held by one caste (or sometimes several). This dominant caste has economic power by virtue of controlling the means of subsistence, and also wields political power on behalf of the king. Its rights over the land may not amount to ownership as understood in an individualistic society, but they are pre-eminent so far as others in the village are concerned. This caste has powers to grant land and to provide employment for members of other castes, together with judicial powers and a virtual monopoly of authority (in the sense that if the village headman is not one of the notables of the dominant caste he must in effect be a tool of theirs if he is to function at all). So far as the dependent castes in the village are concerned 'their members obtain direct or indirect access to the means of subsistence through personal relationships with the members of the dominant caste in virtue of the functions which they are fit to perform and which the dominant caste requires'.[3]

In the context of the study of social stratification in general, are we justified in regarding the caste system we have outlined as lying at one extreme of a continuum of stratification types of which the arrangements in western societies lie at the other end? And more specifically is the Negro/White situation in the southern states of the United States of America to be regarded as coming into the same category as caste in Hindu India? There are a number of related factors which individually and collectively would suggest that the answer to both these questions is 'no'. First, the Indian caste system is a product of the widespread acceptance,traditional in its setting, of values and beliefs implying a fundamental human inequality and of the rightness of a hierarchical view of society. Such a system would be totally incongruent where even lip service was paid to the Christian ethic and to the individualistic ideals of nineteenth-century philosophers. Secondly, one should stress that what we find traditionally in Hindu India is an internally consistent caste system, where the constituent parts are logically related to the whole. A situation where one group (Negroes) has in theory equality of rights with all other members of society but is effectively denied some of these rights in practice, obviously involves fundamental inconsistencies for which there is no parallel in traditional Indian society. Thirdly, before a pattern of the Indian type could be reproduced in another setting, status and power would have to be completely dissociated from each other in a manner comparable to that of the Brahmin/Kshatriya relationship. In fact this disjunction is not found elsewhere; the ruler has not been deprived of his religious prerogatives. As Dumont puts it 'the supremacy of the priest is an Indian fact which has remained unexportable: India has exported quasi-caste rather than caste proper'.[4] The unique feature of the traditional Indian situation is that though the Brahmin is spiritually supreme he is materially dependent; yet on the other hand, though the king is in a dominant position materially, he occupies a subordinate position spiritually.

Though we can readily find, therefore, in the United States and elsewhere particular features of the way people behave in relation to each other which seem to bear close resemblance to some of the historical characteristics of social interaction in India, it would be wrong to use the term caste or caste-like to describe these, since essential elements are missing. Would it be truer to say that when *distinction* between fairly closed status groups has been done away with legally (as with the abolition of slavery) and is no longer in tune with prevailing values and beliefs, religious and other, unofficial *discrimination* is apt to come in as a replacement, perhaps to satisfy some human need, particularly in conditions of stress where certain groups feel their position is threatened? Are the inconsistencies we find in egalitarian societies a resurgence of what was more openly catered for in hierarchical societies? Is Dumont right when he says, 'In the modern age hierarchy has become "social stratification", that is hierarchy which is shame-faced or non-conscious, or as it were repressed'?[5]

To what extent has the caste system in India outlived its usefulness, and to what extent have recent developments shown that such a way of ordering social relationships is incompatible with the needs of modern society? If one were to give an affirmative answer to such questions it would be natural to point to untouchability having been declared illegal, to the outlawing of practices such as the burning of widows and abandonment of children, to the spread of western forms of property rights, and to the increasing importance of the market in economic affairs. On the other hand, tentatively negative answers could be supported by evidence showing (*a*) the remarkable ability of the Hindu caste system to survive territorial conquest and overlordship by adherents of monotheistic religions whether Islamic or Christian; (*b*) the importance of the safety valve provided by renunciation and the formation of new religious sects, which, when they ceased to admit recruitment from outside, themselves became castes; (*c*) the strengthening of small local castes by their amalgamation in wider territorial groupings, and so on. By a number of processes—rejection, mixture, combination—caste society has proved itself able to adapt to many aspects of social change.

In short, we cannot say what the future of the Indian caste system may be. What we can say is that in its long history it provides important lessons in the ordering of social relationships both on a local and on a societal level, and that our failure to benefit from these lessons has certainly been due in large part to the abhorrence which many of the practical applications of the pure/impure dichotomy created in the minds of men who had internalised egalitarian beliefs and values, the difficulties in the implementation of which are only now becoming fully apparent.

FEUDAL RELATIONSHIPS

Feudal relationships were characteristic of periods when the central authority was weak and disorder rife, and when people therefore desperately needed the protection of those more powerful than themselves who were near at hand.[6] It was essentially a chain of personal relationships (sometimes, but not always, blood relationships) on the one hand, and relationships of dependence and obedience, and of services rendered on the other, stretching from the highest to the lowest. Though the lowest were in a position which by modern standards would be regarded as extremely unfavourable, they were serfs rather than slaves. That is to say they were personally free but were tied to the land, in that they had to get consent to leave the land; they could not be sold as slaves were sold, but when the land was transferred they went with it. In one sense indeed it was partly the absence of a large class of slaves that made necessary the creation of relationships that are characteristically feudal. We should note that the legal position of the serf, though better than if he had been a slave, was nevertheless inferior to and different from that of his master, so that as with slavery we have here a set of social arrangements in which there were marked inequalities in the legal rights of different categories of people. At the other end of the chain the dominant class was a class of full-time warriors by profession who took no part either in agricultural activities or in trade, but whose revenues derived from the land they held, from the tolls and dues they were able to exact and from the spoils of war, and who exercised legal authority over others. Looking at the structure as a whole, the relationship was essentially an exploitative one, the principal beneficiaries being the warriors, though society was also able in this way to support a body of priests and monks. Land was central to the whole system. The relationship between a vassal and his lord, for example, was usually, though not invariably, in the form of the latter allowing to the former rights over a parcel of land, the fief (involving tenancy and not ownership), in return for sworn loyalty and faithful performance of services both military and other.

Although at the time of the French Revolution feudalism and the existence of a nobility were thought of as inextricably intertwined, this was, in fact, a feature of the *later* stages of the development of the system in Europe. In the earlier phase, from the ninth century to the twelfth, there had not been a noble class in European society, if by this we mean a class with a legal status of its own which was hereditary, save in special circumstances governed by formal rules. The dominant families of that day could not lay claim to high status ancestry. It was not until the thirteenth and fourteenth centuries, marked as they were by increasingly frequent revolts against the nobility, that lineage and legal status first characterised the upper layer of society, and that stratification assumed a rigidity much greater than either before or since. This was the period when certain features of knightly life which have become very familiar to us were at their height. Increasing legal differentiation between the classes or 'estates' developed. Laws tended to impose ever greater restrictions on the bearing of arms by the lower orders. The nobility, predominantly living in the country rather than the towns, had a mode of life which was quite distinctive. Estate management, and even more participation in any agricultural activity, was for others. Apart from the profession of arms and carrying out of the appropriate judicial duties, their leisure pursuits (such as hunting and tournaments) were also specific to their class. And as time went on their rules of conduct became increasingly precise and refined; concepts such as courtesy, chivalry and courtly love made their appearance (at least in the literature) more and more frequently.

It is not difficult to see that feudal types of relationship, and the accompanying kind of stratification pattern, were bound to become less and less viable as centralisation of authority increased, as land ceased to be the only important factor, as a money economy developed and the scope for trade and industry widened, as new forms of power replaced water and human power, and as the invention of gunpowder gradually rendered the fully equipped warrior on horseback obsolete. Neither the attempted complete exclusion from the nobility of all who were not already of noble birth, nor permitting rich merchants to join the knightly circle by acquisition of land or by intermarriage, could do more at best than postpone very temporarily the loss of the privileges and power of a dominant class that no longer had any real basis for its pre-eminent position.

PART TWO

Avowed equality yet widespread inequality: Britain and the United States

Introduction 2

In the early part of chapter 1 we drew attention to a fundamental distinction between societies in which there was supposed to be basic equality of treatment as between all adult males and their families, and societies in which there was deliberate *inequality* of treatment at least in certain vital respects. Taking contemporary Britain and the United States as examples of the first type of situation we must begin by discussing a few fairly general points. Our concern in this and most of the following chapters is with two contemporary advanced capitalist societies both of which are regarded as being characterised by ideologies embodying liberty and equality as basic features. There is perhaps need to remind ourselves of the comparatively recent nineteenth-century origins of these values, but it is more important to consider what some would regard as their inherent contradictions. One of these has been neatly put by Dumont: 'In effect, if the whole of humanity is deemed present in each man, then each man should be free and all men are equal. . . . By contrast, as soon as a collective end is adopted by several men, their liberty is limited and their equality brought into question.'[1] Again, it is not unfair to contrast the theory of a social contract whereby an individual is supposed to enter society of his own free will and with particular ends in view on the one hand, and the widely accepted reality that individual consciousness is in fact shaped in the course of socialisation on the other hand. Small wonder then that we find in these societies such a startling contradiction between their proclaimed egalitarian values and the gross inequalities which can be seen to characterise virtually all aspects of social life within them.

An important corollary is that in Britain and the United States grave difficulties arise in any attempt to achieve agreement in identifying the particular groups who are receiving unequal treatment in some meaningful bundle of respects. If you start from a base line of inequality associated with particular criteria, then it becomes a *relatively* simple question to say which groups of people will be unequally treated in matters such as their legal, political and basic human rights. If, on the other hand, your base line presupposes equality of treatment, at least as between adult male citizens in these respects, all societal guide lines for the delimitation of classes, status groups and the rest at once vanish, and a case can be made out not merely for differing on the precise boundary lines between such groups, but even for denying the very existence of any groupings of the kind worth studying at all. Indeed, once you have nominal equality before the law, universal manhood suffrage, and lip service paid to egalitarian values, then sooner or later superfically plausible statements such as 'We are all middle class now' are sure to gain currency, particularly in periods when the general level of incomes is rising.

From the very wide range of possible types of structured inequality we propose to select in the first instance three groups, those that are economic in character, those relating to power and those concerned with status. These, of course, are the three dimensions which have tended to dominate discussion ever since Weber made out a case for a multidimensional rather than a unidimensional approach to problems of social stratification. After this has been done we shall, in chapter 8, examine the case for and against thinking in terms of a number of dimensions of this kind, and also the interrelationships among them. In the three following chapters we shall examine some other important types of structured inequality—in life expectancy, in access to educational and career opportunities, and in access to housing. Then in chapter 12 we look at some of the more important types of attitude and behaviour which can be shown to have particularly strong links with some of the kinds of inequality we have been looking at. Chapter 13 is devoted to a consideration of the problems that arise from the widely differing constructions of reality that may characterise different individuals and groups. In chapter 14 we look at the nature, the changing extent and the consequences of movement up and down the social scale. And in chapter 15 we explore another and vitally important dimension of social stratification, namely sexual stratification. In the past it has been all too common in sociological discussion either to ignore the significance of sexual divisions in society altogether, or to relegate references to them to footnotes or afterthoughts. Sexual stratification is, however, now recognised as a valid and significant component of the study of social stratification; and the fact that in the ordering of chapters this theme appears late in the sequence, carries no implication of lesser importance than the issues dealt with at an earlier stage.

Then in chapter 16 we examine or re-examine some of the more contentious issues of current debate in the 1980s. And finally, by way of comparison and contrast to the position in the two advanced capitalist societies we have been considering, there is a necessarily brief discussion of the corresponding situation in state socialist societies.

Differing theoretical orientations 3

As the study of social stratification and social mobility is merely part of the wider study of society, it naturally follows that the whole range of possible theoretical models and methods of approach is equally applicable to the part as to the whole. In a book of the present kind it would clearly be both inappropriate and impossible to attempt to give an account of many of these. Instead, all that will be aimed at in the present chapter is somewhat arbitrarily to select four differing theoretical perspectives particularly closely associated with stratification studies, and to give a very brief account of the special relevance of each of them to this particular field.

MARX[1]

Marx's theory of class was not intended to be an explanation of the particular social stratification pattern in England, Germany or anywhere else at the time he was writing. It was part of a theory aimed at explaining how historical change from one type of society to another had come about and would continue to come about. Thus feudal societies had given way to capitalist societies because a rising middle class of capitalists successfully struggled against a feudal landed aristocracy and won the day. This merchant and industrialist class in effect then merged with those whose property consisted of land to form a new capitalist class, and those whom they were exploiting (by squeezing from them as much as possible of the surplus value created by their labour power) formed the working class. The intermediate strata who were not entirely dependent for their livelihood either on working for someone else or on employing others, the petty bourgeoisie and the peasantry, would when capitalism reached its crisis have to join forces (however reluctantly) with one or other of the two opposing classes between which polarisation would by then have taken place. In the meantime, their existence certainly blurred the otherwise clearcut distinction between the bourgeoisie proper and the proletariat, the owners of the means of production and the propertyless masses with nothing to lose but their chains.

In this model of capitalist society on its way to ultimate replacement, after a class struggle, by a very different form of society, there could only be two classes in the true sense of the term. Membership of one or other depended primarily on very specific economic criteria (relationship to the means of production), though other elements (e.g. type of alienation) were also involved. And for a class 'in itself' to become a class 'of itself' (that is, for a mere aggregate of people similarly situated to be ready for concerted political action either in defence of the *status quo* or to overthrow it) there had to be the additional subjective element of 'class consciousness', including a distinct ideology, a particular view of the world and a common programme of action. In all of this, it is important to notice, the distinction between manual and non-manual work, which has tended to loom large in recent discussions of social stratification and social mobility, has no place at all; nor, of course, have purely status criteria.

A great deal has been written since Marx died about the predictive value of his approach. Did he, for example, understate or overlook the emergence of the so-called 'new middle class' of managers, professional people and others? He certainly predicted an increase in the number of what he regarded as 'unproductive workers' in the later stages of capitalism, but their position in the production process would make them members of the proletariat rather than of intermediate strata, who could in any case (because of their ambivalent position) not fulfil the criteria for being a true class in the Marxian sense. Has his analysis been proved faulty because of the long delays that have taken place in the overthrow of capitalism, or because where it *has* been overthrown the preceding class struggle (and the outcome) does not seem to be in close accord with the pattern he postulated? It hardly seems worth while for our present purpose to engage in what has tended to become a rather sterile and inconclusive debate on issues of this kind. It is perhaps more important to point out that the usefulness of the Marxian model in understanding what goes on in contemporary capitalist societies is still widely accepted. It may need adaptation to meet some of the changes that have taken place since his day by, for example, using control of, rather then simply ownership of, the means of production as the important criterion. But in its essentials it remains virtually without serious rivals as an internally consistent system for analysing capitalism and its immediate predecessors.

WEBER[2]

For Marx, as we have seen, ownership of the means of production meant power over others. The capitalist/worker dichotomy, though basically an economic one, did not need, as he saw it, to be supplemented by separate classifications on the basis of power, prestige or anything else, since once you knew who the capitalists were you also knew who the oppressors were and who held the reins of power. Weber, on the other hand, could not accept the adequacy of a unidimensional approach to problems of social stratification, he saw no reason why polarisation should occur. The economic order constituted, in his view, only one of the important dimensions to be considered. There were probably at least two others of significance, which have been most usually described by subsequent writers as first, the status (or social honour) dimension, and secondly that of power (or party). Despite there often being considerable common ground in practice, it was nevertheless desirable to keep these three analytically distinct from each other.

In the economic order there was some resemblance between Weber's formulation and that of Marx in that the basic criterion in defining relationships and in distinguishing classes was that of possessing property or not possessing it. Weber did not, however, see the situation in Marxian terms as a dichotomy between a propertied and a propertyless class with transitional intermediate strata. He seems on the contrary to have had in mind four principal class groups: a dominant class based on ownership of business and property, a white-collar class without property, a petty bourgeois class and a manual working class. In the same way as Marx had done, he saw that before conflict between classes could take place, a high degree of class consciousness would have to have developed within each of the relevant groupings.

Weber's status order depended basically on how someone's behaviour was evaluated by other members of the community and may be thought of as often, though not always, being local rather than national in scope. The status groupings that have tended to emerge from field studies claiming to be, or appearing to be, in the Weberian tradition have tended to be not less than five or six in number. And Weber's ideas on the power or party dimension are sometimes interpreted as envisaging a continuum rather than a dichotomy or a hierarchy of groups.

Weber's approach to problems of social stratification has certainly had a major influence on the very large number of American investigations in the 1940s and 1950s. It is unfortunate, however, that as we shall see later, relatively little empirical work has been done to follow up his suggestions regarding the possible societal significance of the presence or absence of congruity between and among the various dimensions of stratification at particular times.

PARETO[3]

Pareto's theoretical contribution to problems of social stratification concentrates on the relation between those possessing power, whom he calls 'the governing elite', and those without it, namely the non-elite. Though in his writings he is highly critical of the Marxian approach, it may be noted that as in the case of Marx his model is essentially dichotomous. Pareto uses another concept of his own, 'the circulation of elites' to describe two processes which though separate are nevertheless in some measure interrelated.

The first is that whereby individuals move from the elite to the non-elite or vice versa, which we more commonly discuss today as social mobility. But Pareto's term also covers a second type of process, whereby a governing elite collapses and is replaced by another. Although he did not devote nearly as much attention to this second process as to the first, he clearly regarded it as very closely linked with the upward and downward movement of individuals (or the lack of it). For in his formulation, governing elites collapse because they have failed to provide an entrée for vigorous new blood from the non-elite sector, and have failed to discard their own dross through fostering the downward movement of other individuals. When circulation is impeded in this way a governing elite clearly becomes ossified and is ripe for replacement by a new governing elite, often by force.

A FUNCTIONALIST APPROACH

In seeking to explain in functionalist terms why stratification exists, we can take as our starting point the statement that different occupational positions require particular kinds of skilled performance. It follows from this that these positions must be filled by people with the necessary ability and training. At this stage an issue of special importance is brought in, to the effect that certain occupational positions are functionally most central to the operation of the given social system. How this centrality is to be shown empirically for any given society is one of the major matters of debate, particularly if this is to be established without some circularity of reasoning. If we suppose, however, that these functionally central positions have been successfully identified, the next statement has to be that the ability to fill these positions and the motivation to train for and undertake them, is unequally distributed throughout the population. Having said this, we are led inexorably to the triumphant conclusion that inequalities of rewards (in incomes, fringe benefits and status) will emerge, sufficient to ensure that the supply of appropriate occupants of these functionally central positions, matches up to society's demand for them.

The last paragraph is a very bald summary of the position taken by Davis and Moore when, in 1945, they first spelt out a basically functionalist approach in their well known article in the *American Sociological Review*, 'Some Principles of Social Stratification'.[4] A storm of controversy ensued and can hardly be said to have entirely died down even now. From this long-drawn-out debate three points can be selected, perhaps somewhat arbitrarily. First of all Wrong, defending Davis and Moore, claimed that their critics had not dented their main contention, which was that in a society with a high degree of division of labour you have to have unequal rewards.[5] If one replaces 'have to have' by 'are likely to find', it would be hard to quarrel with this proposition. But the argument then shifts to two further interrelated questions—how unequal need the rewards be, and can the actual inequalities of any *particular* society's reward structure be explained/justified in functionalist terms? Our own answer to the second of these questions is 'No', as will be explained later in chapter 4.

Secondly, Tumin suggested that talented people are often influenced by factors other than material rewards in their career decisions, and that reward structures of the types with which we are familiar have dysfunctions so far as ensuring that important positions are satisfactorily filled.[6] Thirdly, many critics pointed out that there was no known way of distinguishing positions of central importance to society from other positions; and that if one assessed their importance by the rewards attaching to them this was clearly inadmissible.[7]

In what follows we shall at appropriate points consider which of these, as well as certain other approaches, either in their original or in a modified form, seem to be most useful in trying to understand the origins, the persistence and the significance of the network of interrelated social inequalities found in the two societies with which we are currently concerned. We do not ourselves believe that some kind of synthesis between what are often referred to as consensus and conflict theories, or some compromise between a unitary and a pluralistic frame of reference, is necessarily completely ruled out, even though there are admittedly major obstacles still to be overcome before this is likely to prove possible. We feel, for instance, that Prandy may well be working on the right lines when he produces evidence to show how in British society views regarding the justification for the existing pattern of social inequality form a continuum.[8] Those furthest from any possibility of improving their occupational position in terms of material rewards and power tend to take a Marxian stance, stressing the complete divergence of interest between classes, and believing that conflict leading to a total change in the structure of society is the only answer. At the other end of the continuum those who have obtained high rewards and are in positions of power, naturally tend to think of social stratification in terms of status groups, where differential rewards and influence are legitimated by the contribution that those in high positions are making to the welfare of society as a whole, and where no divergence of interest between the groups is involved. In between these two extremes, people incline towards a status or a class view according to where they see themselves in the occupational hierarchy and how they rate their chances of improvement.

Economic inequality 4

The unequal distribution of income and wealth is the foundation of the sociological concept of class. Contemporary approaches to social stratification all begin from Marx's or Weber's analyses. Radically divergent at some levels (see chapter 3), both accord the possession and distribution of economic resources a crucial role in determining position in the social order. Not all concur with this view, though. Dahrendorf, for example, takes the distribution of authority to be the decisive variable in the stratification systems of advanced industrial societies. Nevertheless, all agree that ranked social groupings, defined according to the level and kind of economic resources possessed by individuals or family units, certainly reflect power and status differences. Power and status, the other basic factors in the operation of stratification systems, are dealt with in subsequent chapters.

Three questions present themselves for discussion here: What is the extent of economic inequality today? What are the causes of the inequality that we observe? Is this inequality of social consequence?

THE EXTENT OF ECONOMIC INEQUALITY

An accurate response to this question is more difficult than it appears. Statistics are abundant, but can be invalid and unreliable, and hence misleading. Some writers have urged that occupational and state pension rights be included in calculations of the distribution of wealth. Indeed, such inclusion narrows considerably the extent of economic inequality: the share of wealth owned by the top 1 per cent of the British population in 1979 drops from 24 per cent to 13 per cent.[1] The traditional definition of wealth, however, is that it comprises marketable assets. Pension rights are strictly speaking non-marketable assets since they are not transferable; calculations which include such assets as wealth are therefore, it is argued, invalid.

Unreliability essentially arises from the understatement of income, for tax avoidance purposes. Media coverage has tended to emphasise the loss of revenue accruing via the 'grey economy' (undeclared income from work carried out 'unofficially'), populated by skilled manual workers and social security recipients. Evidence clearly shows, however, that understatement of income is much more significant amongst higher-income groups. There are, in any case, many perfectly legal ways of reducing one's tax load: deductible expenses, salary increases in the form of fringe benefits, loss-making 'cover' businesses, distribution of capital and property amongst the kinship group, etc. Add to this, illegal tax avoidance and the differential effect of indirect taxes[2], and the progressive taxation systems of both Britain and the United States fall into disarray. A 1976 US Internal Revenue Service report noted that 250 persons with annual incomes over $200,000 p.a. paid no income taxes at all; Americans falling into the top income bracket pay on average only 60 per cent of the taxes they should on paper be remitting. The consequence is that *proportionate to income*, the less affluent pay more taxes than do the rich; this trend has intensified over the years as a consequence of rising rates of indirect taxation and inflation[3]. Currently in Britain, the top 10 per cent of earners pay 24 per cent of their income in direct taxes; the bottom 10 per cent pay 15 per cent.[4] In proportion to their original incomes, the worst-off pay more (see below).

It can safely be concluded that for both the United States and Britain, inaccuracy in the statistics on the distribution of income and wealth usually means understating rather than overstating the extent of inequality.

THE DISTRIBUTION OF INCOME

Measured in terms of real purchasing power, general living standards have risen throughout this century, though not always smoothly or continuously. *Inequalities* in the distribution of income remain substantial, though modification has occurred, taking place more markedly in some periods than others. It seems that significant changes took place during the period 1938–45, but that since 1960 or so there has been no further narrowing in the range of income inequality in Britain.[5] In the United States, the richest fifth of American families receive over 40 per cent of national income before tax; the poorest fifth receive 5 per cent. This distribution has not changed significantly since 1945.[6] Taxation and cash benefits do make a difference, but not as much as is even officially intended. In Britain, redistribution of known income through the combined effects of taxes and benefits (taking the size of households into account) leaves the top 10 per cent of households with an annual income 51 per cent higher than that of the bottom 10 per cent.[7] The benefits of whatever redistribution has occurred are agreed to have left the relative position of the majority of the population unchanged. Whilst the share of the very richest has declined, the share of the lower 50 per cent has remained stable.

The distribution of income by occupational group has, however, changed somewhat. At the risk of over-generalisation, routine non-manual and lower-level professional workers have lost some ground relative to skilled manual groups. There is certainly a degree of overlap between the earnings of skilled manual and lower-level non-manual jobs, but this fact has been overdrawn. On the whole, differences in income levels between the manual and non-manual sectors remain. In 1979, the average gross hourly rate of pay for a British adult male manual worker amounted to only 69 per cent of that awarded to his non-manual peer—including overtime rates.[8] It is often forgotten in this context, furthermore, that expansion in the non-manual sector since 1945—used to support the thesis of increasing equality in the distribution of income via greater opportunities in more highly-rewarded occupations—has importantly consisted of an explosion of positions at the *routine* non-manual level. These vacancies have been overwhelmingly filled by women, whose earnings are still considerably less than those of men at all levels. The much-vaunted overlap in manual/non-manual earnings is not, therefore, a reflection of significantly increased class equality, but an admission of persistent *sexual in*equality.

THE DISTRIBUTION OF WEALTH

Wealth is even more unequally distributed than is income. Its distribution is regarded as central to the discussion of economic inequality for two main reasons. Firstly, wealth is inheritable, and thus contributes to the perpetuation of economic inequality; and secondly, possession of marketable assets in sufficient quantity is a powerful lever in access to social and political power and privilege. This latter point is touched upon later in the chapter; the former is discussed here.

In both the United States and Britain, the self-made man is held up as an example of equality of opportunity. Yet even in America, the facts belie the folk-tales: there *are* self-made men—and even a few self-made women—but they are exceptions. Wealthy parents produce wealthy children, as countless studies show; and over time, it has become *more* difficult to amass a fortune on the scale of those collected by the early industrial entrepreneurs such as the Carnegies, the Rockefellers, and so forth.

There has been a long-term reduction in the concentration of wealth among the very richest. Whilst the Wall Street crash in 1929 and the ensuing Depression may well have started the ball rolling, other factors are considered to have been more influential in recent decades: home ownership has increased enormously, and property prices have risen faster than securities and share prices. Nevertheless, in the early 1970s the wealthiest 20 per cent of Americans owned three-quarters of the nation's assets, and the wealthiest fifth of the British could claim over 80 per cent of the nation's wealth as their own.[9] In the face of such a skewed distribution, it is fair to ask whether the ownership of a British semi-detached or an American suburban home makes much more than a cosmetic difference to the extent of economic inequality.

PROGRESS ON THE ROAD TO EQUALITY?

The most generous interpretation of the data on economic inequality, then, is one of mild, cautious optimism: inequalities *have* been reduced, especially in the distribution of income. Yet the scale of the modifications has not been dramatic or even continuous; and poverty has in no way been eliminated. Rather, the evidence points to the emergence of an 'underclass' since 1945. The underclass consists of individuals and households characterised by at least one social 'stigma' (a socially disadvantageous attribute) and locked into a web of poverty, blocked opportunity and naked exploitation. They are members of 'minority groups' in the sociological sense of the term: for example, women, minority ethnic groups, the old, the handicapped.[10] Those who cannot work or cannot find employment are consigned to dependence upon (usually inadequate) government benefits or upon family members; those actually in the labour force are likely to be relegated to insecure, ill-paid jobs offering little or no opportunity for promotion or upward mobility. In other words, they are consigned to the *secondary sector* of what is called the *dual-labour market*.[11]

Giddens has argued that the operation of the dual-labour market is the main factor which separates the underclass from the mainstream of the working class. Prejudiced attitudes towards minority group members may act to create a 'buffer zone' preventing upward mobility for the underclass, in that such attitudes may be more common amongst those (i.e. sectors of the working class) who feel themselves to be most directly in competition with this group on the labour market.[12] In America, blacks and latterly Hispanics have been major sources of secondary sector labour. In Europe, the underclass has been typically imported: in the case of Britain, it has been Commonwealth immigrants who have filled this function. Women, of course, have in all cases furnished a constant 'reserve army' of labour for the secondary sector.

THE CAUSES OF ECONOMIC INEQUALITY

In a society predicated upon legitimate competition for potentially unequal shares of finite resources, some individuals will succeed at least partly by virtue of personal qualities and circumstances. If for example, the principal breadwinner has more native talent, a stronger physical constitution, greater good fortune and a tendency to work harder than his fellow men, these features may contribute to his family's larger income; though we must, of course, remember that his industrious habits may be social rather than personal in their origin. Again, the size and structure of the breadwinner's family clearly have some bearing on its relative poverty or affluence—how many other breadwinners there are, how many dependants and so on. But these 'personal' factors are of small moment in comparison with the *social* factors which cause economic inequality. Furthermore, personal and social factors are interrelated. For example, success at school and high scores in IQ tests are interpreted as signs of high intelligence. Yet these variables are heavily correlated with social class membership too. There is no real basis for the belief that intelligence is unequally distributed by social class. On the contrary, it is known categorically that working-class children underachieve at school, and that IQ tests are vulnerable to cultural bias and educational environment (see chapter 10).

Lenski has pointed out that economic differences as a basis for hierarchical social rankings operate only when a society produces a surplus – i.e. goods which are not necessary for the survival of its people.[13] Inequalities in the distribution of surpluses occur in the majority of societies, though institutionalised means of redistribution exist to a greater or lesser extent alongside. (In modern western societies, fiscal policy and welfare measures have this function.) The specific causes of economic inequality in a society vary according to its mode of production, which in turn is related to social structure and process. In capitalist economies, economic inequality stems from two 'rules of the game': private ownership and the free market. Private ownership of the means of production justifies the unequal distribution of profits; market forces determine the value of different kinds of labour. Government intervention via taxation and policy initiatives may mitigate the more extreme manifestations of inequality that emerge, by setting limits upon market forces (for example, minimum wage legislation) and upon profit levels (for example, by controlling monopolies). No western government has, however, completely *changed* the rules of the game—for example, by prohibiting the transmission of wealth between generations. The market ideally seeks the best labour at the lowest cost. Economic and social variables can and do influence the power of the market in this respect. In times of full employment, labour is a scarce commodity and commands a higher return. On the other hand, where more women crowd a narrow range of occupations on the labour market, the cost of their labour will—all other things being equal—remain depressed.

INCOME DIFFERENCES AMONG OCCUPATIONS

That the formulation of sociological theory can be influenced by prevailing social ideology is well demonstrated by the functionalist perspective on social stratification (see chapter 3). Satisfactory performance of certain occupational roles is assumed to be of central importance to system maintenance, and thus to social survival. The major function of social stratification, then, is to motivate the small numbers of able persons available to fill these positions to do so. Such occupational roles require protracted periods of rigorous training and education; they demand a high level of commitment, time and energy. Motivation is assured through the rewards offered: both financial, in the form of high salaries, and social, in the form of job security, good working conditions and high prestige. This perspective also explains why some less skilled or unskilled occupations receive higher rewards than would be expected: the conditions of work may be so undesirable that too few would enter such positions without adequate incentive. The classic example is that of mining, which commands both a high salary and a goodly measure of respect in comparison with other manual occupations.

In that this perspective appears to fit the actual reward system of industrial societies, and supports the commonly-accepted principle of individual reward in proportion to individual effort and merit, it has much initial appeal. Yet the theory is flawed. First, in a complex society in which all are dependent upon others for essential goods and services, who is to say which functions are more central than others? Second, incentives do not necessarily play a significant role in occupational choice; false conclusions are here too easily drawn. For example, although the medical profession in the United States is undeniably reward-oriented, Becker's study of American medical students showed that many had chosen their future occupation for idealistic reasons. As their training wore on and they came into contact with practising physicians, their idealism waned and they became money and prestige oriented. In other words, they had been exposed to a professional socialisation process, which modified their original motivations.[14]

Third, the scarcity of recruits to high-status, highly-paid positions is illusory. The advantages enjoyed by their incumbents are at least partly a consequence of deliberate manipulation, achieved by erecting barriers to access (e.g. high entry qualifications, long periods of training, quotas) and attempts to attain a monopoly (e.g. certification to practise being under the control of the professional association, stipulation of fee scales, and prohibition of advertisement). The potential benefits to be gained by such strategies are so attractive that attempts to claim 'professional status' have multiplied in recent decades—for example, on the part of social workers, schoolteachers and computer programmers, to name but a few. The vital question as to *how much* of the income of people in particular professions is attributable to the artificial limitation of the supply of entrants has been explored by a number of writers. As early as the

1930s a British economist, H. D. Dickinson, made a special study[15] of what he called 'institutional revenue' arising in this way, and showed that one of the most popular and effective devices was to raise the level and broaden the range of subjects in which future would-be entrants must demonstrate their competence, far beyond the point genuinely required for the successful performance of their work roles. The pinnacle of success in professionalism of this kind is reached when statutory authority is obtained so that it becomes illegal for anyone to practise the craft who does not fulfil these conditions, including the successful completion of a long and arduous education and training. An American sociologist, Randall Collins, has recently given some interesting examples where it can be shown that the educational requirements of occupations have been artifically inflated with no corresponding improvement in work performance.[16]

Moreover, these strategies are by no means limited to the professional sector. Practitioners of skilled manual trades have a long tradition of attempting to maintain scarcity in order to ensure a high price for their labour, going back as far as the medieval guilds. One of the main concerns of the skilled trade unions in the First World War was what was termed 'the dilution of labour': if women were permitted to practise such trades as part of the war effort, this would in the long term depress wages, since female labour was plentiful and cheap. In fact, the long-standing exclusion of women from many trade unions can be traced back to fears of this nature. In the manual sector as a whole, collective bargaining and strike action have been instrumental in improving the incomes of the working class, and the question of maintaining or restoring 'differentials' has been of significant concern in the jostling for position on the income hierarchy.

THE SOCIAL CONSEQUENCES OF ECONOMIC INEQUALITY

In direct terms, the affluent can clearly enjoy a more comfortable, pleasant and relaxed life than can the less well-off where both living conditions and lifestyle are concerned. The expansion of social welfare provision has not banished the reality that money can still buy vital services. In Britain, private medical practice remains, so that those who can pay for it gain access to speedier, if not necessarily always superior, medical attention. Money can buy immediate access to consultants and can secure priority on non-urgent surgery lists. In Britain debate continues to rage over the presence of pay-beds in state hospitals. It is argued on the one hand that this reduces the facilities available to NHS patients, while defenders of the current position claim that pay-beds generate income for, and attract high-quality medical staff to, the state system. In the United States, disparities in access to treatment are notoriously extreme: estimates suggest that 20 per cent of Americans have no health insurance; for those who do, extent of coverage is closely linked to income level, so that a sizeable proportion of families have inadequate hospital insurance cover.[17]

The *indirect* consequences of economic inequality are at least as significant. Runciman's concept of relative deprivation furnishes a simple example.[18] In modern western societies, social status and self-respect are intimately connected with material affluence; individuals are encouraged to strive for more than they already have. For many, a sense of deprivation may well ensue, resulting from the comparison of one's own situation vis-à-vis the perceived 'average citizen' or those more affluent than oneself. It is by no means necessary to be poor in any absolute sense to experience this feeling (although consumption patterns of the poor may well be deleteriously influenced); a sense of dissatisfaction, depression and loss of self-respect can strike all—except, presumably, the very rich.

Unequal access to educational and occupational opportunities is perhaps the most complex and far-reaching of the indirect effects of economic inequality; as such, it merits and receives separate treatment (see chapter 10). Discussion in the present chapter will restrict itself to two further kinds of indirect effect: inflation, and the influence of the economic élite in social and political life. Both are topics of current debate, the former being a novel formulation, the latter because it is central to the character of the interrelationship between class and power.

INFLATION

It has been argued[19] that inflation is caused by conflict between interest groups over the distribution of resources. Those who control a disproportionate share—those in power—attempt to deceive others claiming a larger share by making spurious financial concessions whilst leaving the distribution of real rewards untouched. The market rapidly adjusts to the new situation by raising prices: the inflation spiral has begun. The more severe the conflict, the more the inflation that is required to hold it in check.

The effects of inflation are unequally distributed too. Those with debts and with assets in non-monetary form do well. This can and has benefited the average home-owner—but it also benefits those running unsuccessful businesses. The attempt to build up financial assets from small beginnings is at a disadvantage, since savings lose value too; those already wealthy suffer less, for their assets tend to be already invested in shares and property. Those dependent upon fixed incomes—typically, socially vulnerable groups surviving on government benefits—lose most heavily via a steady decline in purchasing power. The real value of state pensions in Britain was maintained and minimally improved during the 1970s, but the value of unemployment benefit decreased towards the end of the decade. Alterations in the social security and unemployment benefit systems since 1980 have taken several different directions, but perhaps the most important change has been the abolition of earnings-related supplement since 1982, which, notwithstanding the slight ameliorative adjustments in the budget of March 1983, is bound to worsen the situation.[20] In the United States, the Reagan administration has advised people to make their own provision for retirement. Reliance on fixed incomes is expanding; unemployment rates have risen dramatically, more young people are remaining in post-secondary education, and the proportion of the population over the age of 65 is increasing.

Goldthorpe has demonstrated from the results of the 1972 Nuffield social mobility study (see chapter 14) that in terms of social origins the British middle class is heterogeneous in composition whereas the working class is homogeneous. From this, he surmises firstly that the working class, undiluted by external recruitment, possesses a 'mature' culture and a stable collective class identity. The opposite holds for the middle class. Secondly, the growing acceptance of egalitarian ideology and rejection of the traditional status order has encouraged the working class to press its claims more strongly in the face of a more fragmented middle class. The outcome is the intensification of class conflict, which has only been amenable to the kind of inflationary solution described above. Working-class demands can only be met in *real* terms in times of economic expansion; but Britain's economy has been in overall decline for a long time. The consequence, then, has been inflation and rising levels of industrial conflict.

However, whilst the outcome is not in dispute, Goldthorpe's causal chain is. For one thing, processes of class structuration in the working class are by no means resolved; for another, as Noble indicated, evidence shows that in France and Sweden—where the working class is less homogeneous than in Britain—levels of political radicalism and class-consciousness are higher.[21]

THE INFLUENCE OF THE ECONOMIC ELITE

The securing of an acceptable standard of living for the average citizen, at least when in employment, has been the scale of the progress made towards economic equality during this century. In Britain these gains have been primarily used to finance higher levels of consumption and the expansion of owner-occupation. How far the average citizen has been able to turn these modest economic gains into effective social and political influence is quite another matter. A measure of collective influence on behalf of the working class has been achieved by trade unionism; but the growth of direct political power exercised through the TUC has shown limited and uneven progress. Critics of this position point to the downfall of the Conservative Government under Edward Heath in 1973–4 and the subsequent Social Contract with the Labour Government as evidence of the political 'clout' of British trade unions. Closer analysis suggests such events to be the exception rather than the rule. In the United States, moreover, the trade unions have never wholeheartedly embraced an overt political brief on behalf of working-class interests.

At the other end of the scale, the picture is quite different. There is no doubt that there is an economic elite in both Britain and the United States.[22] Industrial wealth is concentrated in a very small number of hands; this trend is sharpening.[23] Debate centres around the following questions. To what degree have professional managers taken over effective control from shareholders? How far do managers' interests diverge from those of shareholders? What connections does the economic élite maintain with the other elite groups?

It has been the increasing complexity and scale of modern industry together with the rise of the joint-stock company which has created the occupation of the salaried manager and in theory created new channels of upward social mobility. As early as the 1940s, these developments were being interpreted as heralding a 'managerial revolution', in which shareholders were losing their traditional powers over industrial investment, policy and administration. This position has continued to be relatively uncritically accepted in the United States, whereas the body of British social scientific opinion has rejected much of the thesis' import.[24] The critics point out that crucial decisions still rest with the board, membership of which usually stipulates a company shareholding, and that most directors and their families *do* own significant blocks of company shares. Family firms are not an extinct species; family groups control a number of large undertakings, e.g. C & A, IBM, Krupp. Management exercises everyday control, but retains a free hand in policy and planning only insofar as it is in accord with shareholders' interests. When shareholders decide to intervene, they have the right to do so. The prevalence of scattered shareholdings in any one company is deceptive: powerful shareholders hold shares in a number of companies, typically interrelated with each other, and quite small blocks of shares can ensure effective control. (Quite how small is a matter of controversy; a figure as small as 5 per cent has sometimes been suggested).

Are managers nevertheless neutral administrators, subscribing to a set of professional ethics and working in the interests of both capital and labour? Of this, there is little solid evidence. What is known is that managers' economic position, at least at the upper levels, is much more akin to that of the capitalist class than to that of the average citizen. Top management has been shown to be primarily recruited from very well-off backgrounds indeed; in private, managers interact socially with the wealthy, not with the workers. Stanworth and Giddens, reporting on the backgrounds of company chairmen in the early 1970s, stress that the mutual accommodation taking place in the latter part of the nineteenth century between the aristocracy and the business class was a remarkable feature of contemporary British social structure and process. This was accomplished via a common socialisation process experienced at public school and Oxbridge. They contend that by the turn of the century the national economic elite had become indistinguishable from other elites in terms of social background and educational experiences.[25] Today, managers may increasingly view their function as professional in nature but, notwithstanding a certain condescension towards the owner-managers of small family businesses, their interests, ideals and lifestyle do not differ significantly from those of shareholders and entrepreneurs. Essentially, managers are employed to protect and to further shareholder interests—by making as much profit as possible—and it is to this group that they are ultimately accountable.

One version of the managerialist thesis holds that although economic power is concentrated in the hands of management, its effective power is limited by increasing government regulation of industry. State intervention has expanded even in the United States since 1945, but evidence suggests that industry has not been seriously hindered by it, and it has very often helped industry considerably. The industrial lobby can and does prevent and hinder unwanted legislation; once on the statute books, moreover, it may not be too difficult to evade. The problems experienced in both the United States and Britain in enacting and implementing environmental protection legislation stand witness to this. Further, business has been consistently aided by massive cash injections to failing companies, and by extensive tax subsidies and concessions.

Nevertheless, it would be wrong to suggest that western governments do not play *any* role in influencing industrial activity. Neither, to take the opposite position, does the economic elite dominate the polity—the business elite is not unitary in any simplistic way, in any case. Giddens suggests that there has been a reduction in the degree to which direct control is exercised by any one elite over any others, and that this has been replaced by the growth of formal mechanisms of mutual influence.[26]

Research into the interconnections between elites is on the upswing. Useem and McCormack argue that in Britain a 'dominant segment' has emerged within the business elite which has assumed a political role on behalf of the capitalist class as a whole. They draw this conclusion after monitoring the activities of a large sample of British directors in the late 1970s: they noted their participation in government, advisory functions for government and non-profit organisations, informal networks and club membership.[27]

All writers in this field are agreed that many aspects of this issue remain unresolved. Progress is slow due to methodological problems and facts are hard to come by. Why? Giddens has suggested that in a society which theoretically supports the principle of equal opportunity, the upper class must remain invisible in order to maintain its control over access to elite positions.[28] And as Stanworth has remarked, elite research is much more difficult than investigating life among the working class: elite members are protected from the inquisitive public (which here includes the sociologist) by a myriad of secretaries and minions—and even by electric fences.[29] (Elites and their interconnections are further considered in chapter 6.)

Finally, it almost goes without saying that, because they represent disparities in one's ability to dispose of generalised purchasing power, economic inequalities (in income/wealth) have naturally tended to be regarded as peculiarly basic, especially after nominal equality of civil, political and legal rights has become an established part of a society's arrangements. In popular usage, dichotomies such as that between rich and poor, the haves and the have-nots, seem always to have been with us, and the term 'class' has been most frequently employed to describe a grouping of people or of families with some economic characteristic in common: ownership of the means of production, the need to work for someone else in order to live, relationship to the market, life chances, particular category of occupation (and therefore likely level of income), and so on. It should be noted, incidentally, that the classic definitions of class (e.g. those of Marx and Weber) stressed the importance of a particular social relationship and not merely the possession of a particular individual attribute. When you have classified people in some such fashion, however, whether in only two or in some larger number of classes, you tend to have a grouping which, though the criterion on which it is based may have been predominantly economic, also reflects in some measure degrees of power (other than just purchasing power) and degrees of status. This raises issues that can now be discussed in the following three chapters.

Power inequality in community and society 5

POWER IN LOCAL COMMUNITIES

An important distinction has to be made at the outset between studies that have thrown some light on the power structure of particular communities, and those which concern themselves with power at a societal level. To take the first of these types, there have been a very large number of local community studies in America, but what seems to emerge from them is such a wide diversity of situations as almost to defy meaningful classification. Apart from the fact that non-governmental control (by business leaders in the main) seemed usually to be more important than governmental control, variety characterised most other aspects of the problem. Thus the pattern of power distribution sometimes took a pyramidal form with one or very few men as the key decision-makers, sometimes a caucus form involving some kind of consensus, real or contrived, amongst a fairly large group of key figures, and sometimes a pluralist form with separate power structures for the different fields of community activity. Many studies of local communities have also been undertaken in Britain, and considerable diversity has characterised the findings here as well, though few of them have been specifically concerned with the power theme. One interesting point does emerge when such comparisons as are possible are made between the situation in similar communities on different sides of the Atlantic. This is that business leaders, who tend to form as many as two-thirds or more of the people with local influence in a United States urban setting, count for very much less in England, where those from other walks of life may equal or outnumber them.[1]

There has, as one would expect, been a great deal of controversy regarding the validity of the basic research design of many of these studies of power in local communities. Can one rely on the *reputation* that particular individuals have for playing a key role in local decision-making? And doubt has also increasingly been expressed as to how far investigation of community power structures is helpful as a contribution towards understanding the situation at a societal level.[2]

POWER IN SOCIETY AT LARGE

When we turn to this more important but also much more difficult area of study, there is a marked paucity of major works to be considered, and attention can be concentrated, so far as the United States is concerned, on two classic and contrasting examples, C. Wright Mills, *The Power Elite*[3] and D. Riesman, *The Lonely Crowd*.[4] We should note at the outset that there is a vital distinction to be made between three possible approaches. Wright Mills can be regarded as following the Pareto tradition (where the non-elite consists of an amorphous mass lacking political consciousness and without either the will or the capacity to overturn its rulers). Riesman, on the other hand, saw instead at the top of the power structure a series of veto groups 'each of which has struggled for and finally attained a power to stop things conceivably inimical to its interests and, within far narrower limits, to start things'.[5] A third line of approach, which has apparently not so far been adopted or found empirically valid by any American observer of that society, would be that of a ruling class in the Marxian tradition, based on ownership/control of the means of production, and opposed by a subject class which sooner or later would become fully conscious of the nature of its subjection and would take the necessary steps to overthrow its rulers.

The Wright Mills formulation has been the centre of a great deal of controversy and, if accepted, would tell us much about the structure of power in an advanced capitalist society. He claimed that America's democratic constitution and official political processes were being bypassed and had become a mere sham. America was, in fact, ruled by a group of men who had risen to the top principally in the economic, military and political sectors of American life. The control that this group had over the lives of American citizens was such as to make principles like 'equality before the law' and 'democratic control' seem a hollow mockery.

We shall be discussing later the evidence in support of the view that in societies of the type we are concerned with there exists a substantial number of powerful sectional or strategic elites. If for the moment we accept that this is the case, it must be pointed out that the transition from a position of *that* kind to acceptance of the existence of a single power elite is a difficult one involving a number of related problems. The first and easiest link to establish is that of communication, sometimes regular and close, between individual members of different elites. Similarity of economic position often leads to similarity of lifestyle, and common socialisation experience (e.g. as a boarder in a leading English public school) is likely to make adult social interaction easier, and to provide a further measure of community of interest. Even if people do meet socially, and even if there are factors likely to make for ease of communication among them, we should be careful to note that this of itself provides no direct evidence in support of so-called 'conspiracy theories' of a ganging-up of leading members of different sectional elites to engage in concerted action involving exploitation of the rest of society.

One historical instance where the link between economic and political elites could be clearly seen in British society was the familiar case in which the owner of the largest industrial undertaking in a particular locality almost automatically became the Member of Parliament representing that constituency in the House of Commons. The fact that this no longer happens does not of course prove that the economic and political elites are now completely divorced. It could merely be that leading members of the business world have discovered more effective but less visible means of exerting political influence than by wasting a lot of their valuable time as Members of Parliament. Indeed, on particular occasions one can often be made aware of the political influence that a particular section of the economic elite is able to exert. When, for example, a powerful industrial corporation wants to exploit the mineral deposits in an area of high amenity value, the first reaction both of the local planning authority and of the central department concerned with the environment may be to disallow this. However, when on appeal the matter is dealt with at Cabinet level the economic interest nearly always seems to prevail, and the political influence at the disposal of particular members of the economic elite becomes visible at least for the moment. On other occasions an important business enterprise may simply go ahead and break some planning requirement, relying on the likelihood that by presenting the relevant political authority with a *fait accompli* the law can be flouted.

Lobbying on behalf of pressure groups of many kinds, including business interests, is an acknowledged if not always welcome part of the political scene, and no one can be in any real doubt that political decisions are not taken in a vacuum and that specific economic or other interests are sometimes able to tilt the balance in their own direction. All this, again, though common knowledge, hardly adds up to convincing proof that particular economic interests, or the economic interest generally, *always* prevail when political decisions affecting them are being taken, regardless of which political party happens to be in power. And to some people at least, proof of permanent dominance of this kind would be a necessary prerequisite of their acceptance of a power elite statement of the Wright Mills type as being true for any given society.

A peculiarly British variant of this model appeared in the late 1950s.[6] Hugh Thomas, who was one of those originally putting this idea forward, has since retracted what he now describes as 'this *simpliste* and to me now unattractive view'.[7] The suggestion was that a group of people, described as 'the Establishment', dominated the most sensitive institutions of British society. Close study of the steps leading up to the taking by postwar

British governments of a number of key political decisions showed, it was claimed, that a small group of prominent people in specified strategic positions had been able to exert a critical influence at crucial moments and turn the scales in favour of the outcome they wanted. It was partly a matter of particular positions and partly of the status of certain individuals regardless of position, and among those who were claimed to be members of an Establishment which functioned irrespective of which political party formed the government of the day, were the Archbishop of Canterbury, the Editor of *The Times*, the Warden of All Souls' College, Oxford, and the Governor of the Bank of England. One element in the prestige of the offices concerned was that they had all been important over fairly long historical periods, and this was clearly a phenomenon specific to the British social scene. Besides intermingling on social occasions, the mechanisms of the process of exerting influence were said to include carefully timed letters to *The Times*.

In a more general formulation of the idea of a ruling or dominant class or group the obvious point to be made is that in an advanced capitalist society of the type represented by Britain or the United States all the major social institutions will be found to operate in the interest of such a group rather than that of society at large. Two examples that readily come to mind are the law and the mass media. With regard to the first of these one does not need to be a Marxist to accept the statement that the legal system in any capitalist society has been deliberately framed with the protection of property as one of its main functions. On the other hand, it is also clear that if we take the case of Britain, the extent to which the owner of land or housing is legally protected at the expense of other interests has, in the last few generations, been very severely curtailed. Thus landlords of housing subject to rent control can no longer secure the return on their investment that would be possible on a free market, and their freedom to evict tenants is very limited; while in the case of trespass the position has been modified to such a degree that the circumstances in which a land owner or land user can successfully invoke the law, operate within very narrow limits. It would not be reasonable, however, to interpret these changes as being sufficiently fundamental or being wide enough in their scope to suggest that the protection of property rights was no longer a major feature of the English legal system.

Turning to the case of the mass media and taking as one example the British Broadcasting Corporation, it is not difficult to demonstrate that, in its handling of contemporary issues such as strikes, the BBC seems to have a perception of reality broadly in line with that of the dominant group in British society. It is equally easy, however, for other observers to find instances in recent BBC programmes, relating both to history and to current events, in which the stance taken seems to them consistent with the presence in that organisation of a small but influential group of people dedicated to the overthrow of society as at present constituted. Accusations of partiality of two opposing kinds naturally provide the BBC with the basis for a claim, if not amounting to proof, of complete *im*partiality. The recent history of the American motion picture industry provides similar examples in which the message being put over by the products of that industry can be seen either as helping to legitimate the position of the dominant class or as being calculated to undermine it.

Another difficulty some people find in accepting that a single societal dominant group in any meaningful sense exists, arises from seeing that different sections of any generalised interest group often appear to interpret their needs as demanding quite different political decisions. On the desirability or otherwise of Britain entering the Common Market for instance, the British economic elite was clearly sharply divided along the lines of the benefits or losses thought likely to arise for different types of economic activity. Or again, in the discussions leading up to the drafting and passing into law of the Industrial Relations Act 1971 it is known that some prominent industrialists were in favour of such a measure while others were very much against it. If one accepts that there is a dominant group with a common interest, instances of the type just quoted have to be regarded as differences of view on tactics or strategy rather than ultimate aims, or on short-term considerations rather than long-term ones. When a real crisis develops in which the fundamental interests of the dominant group are seen to be genuinely threatened, all these apparent sectional differences will be forgotten, we are told, and the underlying unity of interest of the group will reassert itself, at least until the immediate crisis is over.

Again, it can be argued that a search for the precise mechanisms by which, for instance, the business leaders of a capitalist economy secure an overall dominance in political decision-making is pointless, since it is self-evident that the institutional setting will ensure that their interests must prevail in the end. Thus in Britain, it is said, both Conservative and Labour governments have to operate within a context where the economic constraints on their actions (whether these show themselves in the form of crises over the balance of payments, over inflation or over mass unemployment) leave them little choice except to resign or to take measures serving the long-term interests of capital rather than labour. The focus of interest, in interpreting the British scene, then shifts to an examination of why it is that a genuinely radical political party has not so far emerged capable of internalising in the minds of the masses an awareness of their true situation and the remedy necessary to transform it. Which brings us back, of course, to the safety-valve and ameliorative measures of advanced capitalist societies to be discussed in a later chapter, and the extent to which they have succeeded in delaying, and may continue to do so, radical changes in social structure and organisation.

In a very real sense, therefore, the only viable model of a power elite or dominant group in a capitalist economy seems to be the Marxian one of a dominant *class* whose interests, however much they may sometimes seem to diverge, lie ultimately in preserving as much as is practicable of the *status quo* of the society in which they are dominant. Perhaps the least satisfactory features of this model are first, the doubt as to whether and if so how far the emphasis needs to be shifted from ownership of the means of production to *control* over them; and secondly, the virtual impossibility of predicting by this approach when the final crisis will occur and what its sequel may be.

The main alternative to a dominant-class model is, of course, a pluralist one. The common features of the various pluralist approaches include hypothesising the existence of a substantial number of separate and largely autonomous strategic or sectional elites, and that interaction among these groups, particularly in the battle to influence the decisions of the political elite, takes place over time with varying outcomes. Such a type of formulation may accord with what we often see taking place in capitalist societies when rival pressure groups attempt to influence political decisions. On the other hand, a major weakness of an approach of this kind is that it generally implicitly or explicitly denies either (*a*) that in the last resort the political decisions reached will tend to reflect the interests of one particular group rather than others, or (*b*) that the institutions of such a society, though they may have suffered modification from earlier stages of capitalism, virtually guarantee such an outcome in the long run.

Power inequality within sectors and occupations 6

It is difficult to quarrel with the broad general statement that in all communities there will tend to be found a number of leadership groups, or with the view that this also holds good of such large and complex units as modern industrial societies. One can go on from there to suggest that while in any society with a large number of elites connected with the different aspects of its life all these leadership groups are of interest, nevertheless some have a much greater societal impact than others, in that what they do and the decisions they make, have particularly farreaching consequences for the members of that society. Suzanne Keller designates the latter *strategic elites* as distinct from mere segmental elites; and she suggests that in studying them we should concern ourselves first with their duties, responsibilities and tasks, secondly with their mode of recruitment, and thirdly with how they are rewarded for adequate performance.[1] Using her criteria, the leaders in the spheres of business, politics, military affairs and the civil service, for example, would clearly qualify as strategic elites. Suppose, then, we take a key occupation fitting this requirement that also happens to have a built-in internal hierarchy. Before we can proceed to study what kind of people reach the top of this hierarchy at any given time in any given society, a number of issues have to be resolved.

1. Above what level in the hierarchy should one concentrate attention? The lower the level to which you go, the more work will be entailed in collecting information about the office holders, and the more doubt there will be about whether they really constitute an elite within that occupation.

2. There is the question whether what is of importance is to study those above a particular rank, or to try to ensure that the net brings in those who have a hand in the most important decisions, regardless of the rank they happen to have achieved. If we are interested in power in this sense, we should clearly try to concentrate on influential people rather than holders of nominally influential offices. Yet the advantages are not all on one side in deciding which of these two policies to pursue. In particular, a study of the people known to be most influential in an occupation at the present time may not make comparisons with earlier periods of time possible, since the information on which to judge who were the most influential people *then* may no longer exist. Concentration on office holders, on the other hand, does enable comparisons over time to be made. But in this case some of the people caught in your net may in fact be less influential than some of those outside the net.
3. Having decided which people in the given occupation it is desirable to study, the next issue is what kinds of information about them ought to be collected. The possible range of types of information is obviously very wide, though in practice it tends to be substantially narrowed down because only certain types of data can be obtained from the respondents or from published sources of material to which access is permitted. So most studies of occupational elites lean heavily on the social and educational background of the people concerned, supplemented by such particulars as age, sex, area of origin, size of family of origin and ordinal position in it, method of entry to the occupation, and so forth. How important or otherwise it is to collect information of this type will naturally depend on what one is trying to discover; this is an issue to which we must return shortly.
4. Having identified the present or past occupational elite, most studies attempt for purposes of comparison to identify the population of new recruits to the occupation from among whom in some sense these elites were selected. Such a comparison is not always as easy to make as it sounds. The only

straightforward case is that where there is only a single route of entry to the broad section of the occupation from which the elite is invariably drawn. In most occupations there tend to be a number of possible routes of entry, and where this is so it becomes virtually impossible to identify or say anything useful about the whole population of those eligible for recruitment to that occupational elite. This difficulty arises wherever, for example, it is possible to bring in someone with no previous experience in that particular field, an outsider, and appoint him directly to one of the top positions. In Britain it is, for instance, not by any means unknown for someone appointed as vice-chancellor of a university not to have had any previous university experience either in teaching or in administration, or for someone appointed as a chief constable not to have served in any capacity in a police force.

Despite these difficulties, studies of elite recruitment do endeavour to throw light on the characteristics of the junior entrants to the occupation from whom *in the main* the holders of high office are ultimately drawn. And where possible they also endeavour to identify an intermediate population of those as it were half way up the occupational ladder. The point of doing both these things is to try to discover how far at either of these two stages in elite recruitment there appears to be a weeding out, from members of the technically eligible population from whom selection takes place, of certain types of people in terms of the characteristics it has been possible to identify. Is there, for instance, a second-class citizen type who succeeds in entering the occupation and even in getting some way up the ladder but who is rarely, if ever, successful in becoming a member of the top group?

5. In some types of occupation it may be possible to make a closer examination of what happens at and before the point of entry to the cadet group from whom most of the occupational elite will in practice be selected. If, for example, there is a selection procedure, we can compare the characteristics of the field of applicants with those of the ones selected. If it is an

occupation which draws very largely on graduates, we can make even further useful comparisons. For it is then possible to take the whole population of graduates and see how far they differ in certain respects from those who seek admission to the occupation we are studying *and* from those who actually succeed in being admitted.

6. If we are very fortunate indeed it may be possible to identify the particular component in the selection process at the point of entry to the cadet group which appears to be responsible for making the sample of those selected differ in identifiable respects (e.g. social and educational background) from the population of applicants.

All this can be made somewhat clearer by discussing the main findings of studies of recruitment to a particular occupational elite, namely, the British Higher Civil Service.

The strategic elite in this case may be taken as those who held very senior administrative posts (above the rank of assistant secretary) in the home civil service in 1929, 1939, 1950 and 1967.[2] In terms of social origin, the proportion of them who came from families with a manual work background showed some increase over most of the period, the percentages for the four dates being 7, 9, 20 and 17; if we only take those with a semiskilled or unskilled manual work background, the figures are nil, 3, 3 and 6. These percentages are, of course, a reflection of the inequality of educational opportunity that persisted over the years when these civil servants were receiving their primary, secondary and higher education. Those relating to the most recent group are, in fact, very similar to the social origin proportions amongst all graduates of British universities in 1960 (excluding medical and dental graduates), though we must remember that not by any means all these civil servants were graduates, or entered the service by the open competition route.

Around three-fifths of them *had* come in by that route, however, and it is therefore of some interest to see how new recruits by these open competitions have recently (in 1968–70) compared with graduates generally in their school and university backgrounds.

Some 38 per cent of the new recruits had attended secondary schools administered by a local education authority; a higher proportion—57 per cent—of the 1960 graduates generally had done so. Taking men only, around 3.5 per cent of the new recruits had been at one of four leading English public schools (Eton, Harrow, Rugby, Winchester), compared with only 1.5 per cent of the graduates generally. And more significantly, perhaps, nearly three-fifths of them, men and women, had been at Oxbridge, as against only a quarter in the case of the graduates as a whole.

The issues involved are complex. Nevertheless, the evidence strongly suggests that the under-representation of certain types of school and university in the field of those hitherto submitting themselves to the open competition was partly (and perhaps largely) due to a belief among potential candidates from the under-represented educational establishments, that their chances of entering by this route were unfavourable. It was probably also partly due to the greater likelihood of both working-class and middle-class students at Oxbridge, compared with other universities, seriously considering the possibility of an administrative career in the civil service. It remains to be seen whether recent changes in recruitment and other matters, resulting from the implementation of some of the recommendations of the Fulton Committee, will lead to a more equitable representation of different types of educational background amongst both candidates and those admitted.

So far we have discussed some of the difficulties that have to be faced in attempting to study recruitment to an occupational elite, and we have also looked at one particular example of the findings emerging from research of this type. The question it is natural to ask next is, what useful purpose is served by this kind of enquiry? The main justification clearly lies in the light that an investigation of this type can throw on the degree of openness of a particular society at a given point in time, and the extent to which this has changed over a period. For though it is true that a study of recruitment to a single occupational elite cannot of itself tell us how open the relevant society may be, if we have the results of a number of such studies we ought to be able to make a broad assessment of the position. When people want to give a tentative answer to the question how far Britain is or is not a society of equal access to occupational opportunity, therefore, the results of research into the recruitment of high ranking army officers, bishops, higher civil servants and other occupational elites are clearly highly relevant, even though they may show a considerable measure of diversity among these and other high status professions.[3]

A closely related question which may well be asked is how beneficial to society it would be to have an occupational elite (or occupational elites generally) which is (or are) broadly representative in terms of social background, sex and ethnic origin of the eligible population from which recruitment takes place. Two reasons at once suggest themselves. First, if the society concerned is one where it is popularly supposed to be the case that there is equality of access to important and interesting jobs as between those, regardless of their origins, who have the qualifications to undertake such work, then it is obviously desirable that the facts of the actual situation should not belie the principle that is supposed to be operative to too great an extent. It can serve little useful purpose to anyone if in the course of their socialisation young people internalise a belief that theirs is a society of equality of opportunity, only to find when they read the results of research into the recruitment of occupational elites that this belief has been unfounded.

A second and equally obvious reason for trying to ensure some measure of representativeness in occupational elites is that of making proper use of the talents available in society. Where high status jobs are not in practice open to able people of low status origin they may be less well performed than could be the case, and society suffers. Or again, where people of lowly origin but high ability are denied access to posts in which they could use their talents effectively, and have therefore to engage in work which fails to 'stretch' or stimulate them, there is a clear waste of potential human resources for society, and frustration for the individuals concerned.

There are certain claims, however, which should clearly *not* be made when trying to show the usefulness of studies of occupational elite recruitment. One of these is the claim that, if the top people in a particular service or profession are properly representative in social origin terms of the population at large, then they will, in their decision-making and their policy generally, behave in ways which reflect the interests and needs of the population as a whole. By contrast, it is sometimes claimed, an occupational elite recruited from a narrow social band will tend to pay regard only to the interests of that particular band instead of to those of society in general. Such claims cannot be substantiated on the kind of evidence commonly obtainable in social research; and there is an inherent improbability in the assumption of a direct linkage between social origin and subsequent behaviour in high office. There are too many examples of aristocrats who, as politicians or statesmen, fought for the interests of the underprivileged, and also of people of humble social origin who, on obtaining high positions, seem bent on destroying the ladder up which they themselves have climbed. It is therefore not unreasonable to ask what difference it makes if the top people in key occupations are predominantly of one kind of social origin rather than another? And the honest answer to such a question must be that the attitudes and behaviour of such a group would not necessarily be altered in any predictable direction by a change in the social background of the office holders.

An illustration may make this point more sharply. Take a hypothetical English occupation to which there is only one route of entry, where entrants come exclusively from one or other of two specified public schools and from one or other of two specified Oxbridge colleges, and where the occupational elite necessarily also comes from a similarly restricted educational background. In such peculiar and unlikely circumstances it would be natural to guess that some form of anticipatory socialisation for that occupation and those elite positions must have taken place at the schools and colleges concerned, predisposing their products to seek entry to this occupation rather than others, and fitting closely with the preferences of selectors both at the point of initial entry and in subsequent selection for elite posts. To validate this guess one would still have to establish (*a*) how homogeneous and of what nature the values and beliefs of the members of the occupational elite in fact were, and (*b*) how far and by what means these particular schools and colleges had internalised the predominant occupational values and beliefs in their students. If this were so even in such an extreme, unlikely and apparently straightforward case, how much the more necessary and unpredictable would validation of this kind be where educational background varied widely.

To admit all this is not to admit that the study of occupational elites is of no value, for the types of justification already discussed form perfectly adequate grounds for undertaking research in this field. Moreover, many of these studies have the additional virtue of being able to show how the changing needs at the top of particular occupations have brought people with different kinds of personalities, skills and interests into positions of power and influence. Among English headmasters, for example, the charisma associated with someone like Arnold of Rugby might be inappropriate in a modern school where administrative talents were more relevant. Studies of bishops suggest that because the Anglican Church today has to rely much more heavily than in the past on the revenue from its property holdings, those with an understanding of and interest in financial management have sometimes tended to replace the scholars or the theologians. Though it is often not too difficult to identify the changing policy needs in the higher reaches of a given occupation and the consequent changes in the interests, outlook and skills of the people who hold the top positions, the issue of personality types is a much more controversial one. Thus, although it has sometimes been claimed that high office in a particular organisation tends to be associated with a particular personality type on the part of the office holder, for example the authoritarian personality, it is usually impossible to discover to what extent this end product (even if satisfactorily demonstrated) is the result of people with given personality characteristics (*a*) being particularly attracted towards jobs of certain types, or (*b*) being selected for such jobs; or whether it results from the holding of specified offices accentuating or developing certain personality features already present in their incumbents.

So, although occupational elite recruitment studies have in our opinion value from a number of points of view, they also have their limitations, and no one would deny that research concerning itself purely with the type of person who reaches high office in an occupation and how he gets there needs to be supplemented by much more difficult investigation of how he behaves when he has reached the top. This naturally raises the difficult issue, touched on already, of the locus of power. Before we devote too many resources to studying how particular people behave in their decision-making, we presumably want to know that the decisions to the making of which we are paying special regard are the important decisions from the point of view of the organisation, the occupation or society at large.

A number of interrelated and very complicated issues arise here. Are the only really significant decisions, as Marxists might claim, those involving the allocation of major capital resources? Or is there a case for including all decisions with an important bearing on the life chances of others? Are we only concerned with decisions of national, rather than local importance? And do those with the specialised technical knowledge needed for preparing the case for top but lay persons to adjudicate upon, really have more influence on what actually happens than their lay superiors, so that it is the technical experts who really have the power and whose characteristics and behaviour we ought to be studying? There is a great deal of evidence to suggest both that someone other than a high office holder may often really be making the decisions for which the latter is nominally responsible, *and* that committee decisions are often made beforehand by a small cabal of which some key members may not even sit on the committee itself.

Ideally we should clearly want to follow a particular sequence in our research. First, identify the key decisions. Secondly, identify the people who have most influence in the making of these decisions. Thirdly, discover why it is that they made these decisions rather than other ones, and what difference it might have made in this connection if they had had different characteristics in terms of social and educational origin, interests, skills and personalities. Fourthly, one would want to know how they had come to be in the key position in relation to making or influencing these key decisions, and what kind of rivals had been weeded out at all critical stages in their upward career progress. Viewed in this way, occupational elite recruitment studies should only be undertaken when the important people whose background and careers were to be examined had first been identified, and this in its turn could only be done after the key decisions and the circumstances surrounding the making of them had been located. It is in this sense that critics have argued with some justification that occupational elite recruitment studies, because they tell us nothing directly about occupational power and its exercise, are not truly a contribution to our knowledge of elites at all. For they may be studying the wrong people; and much of the information collected, even if it relates to the *right* people, has no obvious and direct bearing on the way the elite actually behaves in the crucial business of decision-making.

Even more difficult to study than the occupational elites dealt with so far, but clearly of major importance is the *economic elite*. Here the identification of people who appear to have certain types of power, rather than merely dealing with office holders (e.g. chairmen and directors of major companies) is crucial. And in practice detailed studies of particular forms of organisation tend to yield more fruitful results than do enquiries of wider scope. We are as yet far from being in the position of being able to say for this or any other society, which group of people actually constitutes the national business or economic elite, though it is more possible to undertake such an exercise at local level. The whole question of those who come into a top bracket in terms of either income or wealth presents problems of its own for the research worker. The mere fact of possessing these very large incomes or this very great wealth would seem to justify treating the possessors of it as forming some kind of elite. Yet as soon as we ask ourselves how much power do such people in fact have, the obvious difficulty arises that this may be thought to depend at least in part on how they *dispose* of their income or their wealth rather than on its magnitude.

It seems to be broadly the case that, despite heavy and steeply progressive taxes on income and on the transmission of wealth, the proportion of Britain's population coming into any given high real wealth bracket has not significantly declined over recent generations, and tax avoidance has clearly played some part in this. Over recent time some families have, of course, moved out of the well-to-do category and others have moved in, but a surprising number of families seem to have stayed in this group over several generations. It is helpful to be made aware of this, but the bearing it has on the study of elites is not always as clear as it might be. Property takes many different forms and income can come from many different sources, and the changing 'mix' of property types and income sources in the millionaire category, inevitably complicates the analysis of the situation. It can, however, at least be said that research on both sides of the Atlantic does not support the popular belief that self-made men form a much larger component in the group of wealthy Americans than they do in the group of wealthy Britons.

Before we leave the question of elites specific to particular segments of society, mention must be made of the *political elite*.[4] As in the other cases there is controversy over how widely the net should be cast. In British society, for example, should this group include all Members of Parliament or ought it to be limited to members of the government? And when we come to consider the recruitment of such an elite we must presumably concern ourselves with how candidates for election are chosen, and from what population of eligible party members they are selected. It goes without saying that it is of importance to know the social and educational background of candidates for election, of Members of Parliament and of members of governments of different political complexions at varying points in time. But, as with the occupational elite studies, we must be careful not to imply that a knowledge of the social and educational background of a Labour candidate or a Conservative candidate, of itself tells us anything about how such a candidate will behave. Finally, because of the extent to which in favourable circumstances higher civil servants can in practice exercise political power, it is sometimes argued that this professional group should also count as part of the political elite.

Status inequality 7

Before we can usefully start to look at inequality in respect of status, it is as well to examine the term itself. As commonly used, it represents an attribute or group of attributes which can attach either to a person or to a position, occupation or office. A second point to note is that it is an attribute conferred by others, and in one sense there is very little that a person or office holder can do to improve his status except by changing the office he holds or altering his behaviour. As the scope for either of these may be very limited, it is fair to say that the most usual situation is that of someone who wishes that the status attaching to his occupation and to the office he holds within it was much higher, but who finds that the rest of the community is slow to modify its evaluation in such matters. A third point is that someone's status in one or more of his leisure pursuits or part-time activities may differ completely from that deriving from his full-time work. A fourth point is that in the course of their lives people often *achieve* a higher status than that *ascribed* to them as youngsters by virtue of their membership of a particular family. Fifthly, it should be remembered that status is not merely an attribute but also implies a particular type of social relationship where deference comes in. Shils prefers to use the term 'deference-position' instead of 'status', and one of the advantages of doing so is that the relationship between the various dimensions of inequality is clarified.[1]

If then we say that the idea of status implies some sort of generally accepted hierarchy of positions and/or people, two major difficulties can at once be seen to arise. First, how can we know that any particular hierarchical pattern is in fact generally accepted, since people may either not think in these terms at all or may take the easy way out by agreeing with any pattern an interviewer may suggest to them. A second major difficulty concerns the degree to which status is independent of the economic and power factors already discussed, if at all. It is obvious that in a Marxian analysis both status and power, or the lack of them, are derived from ownership or non-ownership of the means of production, and that therefore it would be pointless to study status separately. And even in Weber's model, very close interrelationships between status ranking and his other two orders are, as we have seen, assumed. Although, therefore, status may in many cases be a mere reflection of elements already considered, there nevertheless remain a sufficient number of other factors which appear to influence mutual status ranking, to justify extended discussion of this type of social inequality.

COMMUNITY STATUS STUDIES

Among the most important examples of studies of social stratification in local communities is the very large group of such investigations made by Lloyd Warner and his associates in the United States in the 1940s.[2] We are justified in examining the nature of these both because they have had considerable influence on other people's work in this field and because they conveniently illustrate some of the crucial issues that arise. In reporting on the first of the enquiries, the 'Yankee City' one, Warner explains that when respondents were asked to rank their fellow citizens in terms of their social standing, the early interviews tended to support the assumption which he himself made, that this status ranking would be a mere reflection of economic criteria.[3] In other words, wealth and high income were characteristic of those who were given high status, and poverty of those at the bottom of the rank order. However, as the investigation proceeded, it emerged that material factors alone were not always the sole criteria. For top community status ranking did not automatically go to the wealthiest citizens, but was found to be restricted to those who in addition to wealth had another attribute, lineage, in the sense that their families had occupied positions of leadership in the local community for some time. This seemed, in fact, to be the only type of case (that is, at the top level) where non-economic factors played a significant part. To many people's way of thinking it would have been useful if the investigators had explored these exceptional instances further, but in fact Warner was led instead to abandon his early assumption altogether. What now seemed to him to be crucial was no longer the relative wealth or income of individuals or families, but rather the extent to which they intermingled socially. Everyone was, therefore, a member of the particular class (and Warner continued to use this term, though traditionally it had been reserved for a grouping based on *economic* criteria) within which most of his intimate social participation in fact occurred.

In his presentation of the results of the 'Yankee City' investigation the inhabitants were then grouped into what became a very well known sixfold social hierarchy, with the upper-upper class at the top (the old and wealthy families) followed by the lower-upper class (the *nouveaux riches*), an upper-middle class of substantial business men and professionals, and a lower-middle class of small business men, clerks and some skilled manual workers. The remainder of the population, including the rest of the skilled manual workers, was allocated either to the upper-lower or the lower-lower class. Criticism of Warner's classification has centred on two factors amongst others—the vagueness of the criteria on which a distinction is made between adjacent classes (with the single exception of the top two), and doubts as to whether this neat categorisation emerged naturally from the information supplied by respondents or was in reality imposed both on the participants and on the data by those conducting the enquiry.

Apart from criticisms of the particular classificatory scheme, the Warner studies have raised other doubts in people's minds. Can we usefully generalise about the American situation as a whole from studies of such a highly local character, as the authors clearly claim that we can?[4] Does the essentially static nature of the picture drawn not present an entirely false impression of timelessness? And the absence of any examination of social mobility in these communities is particularly strange in the light of Warner's own acceptance of the view that such mobility is of vital importance in examining class systems. Then there is the practical limitation that investigations of this kind can only be undertaken in relatively small communities, since mutual ranking would be impossible otherwise. It was to attempt to meet this last objection, as well as the needs of intercommunity comparison, that Warner and his associates later developed an Index of Status Characteristics (occupation, source of income, house type, dwelling area) by which means, it was claimed, allocation to classes could be done on an 'objective' basis.[5]

What Warner and his co-authors have provided, then, are essentially accounts of the status groupings of specific small American communities at the time the investigations took place. They tell us nothing directly about the structure of power. They throw little light on how the situation described has come about, or on factors likely to lead to social change in the future. As one critic points out, their implications are essentially conservative— 'a stable status hierarchy where the only problem concerns the adjustment of individuals to the existing arrangements and their chances to improve their personal position'.[6]

A STATUS HIERARCHY OF OCCUPATIONS

Status studies covering areas larger than relatively small communities being virtually ruled out in terms of feasibility (and of doubtful value even were this not so), studies of the relative prestige of different occupations have tended to be used as in some sense the counterpart on a societal level of what Lloyd Warner and his associates did at a local level.

One of the pioneer studies in this field was conducted by North and Hatt in 1947 for the National Opinion Research Center in the United States.[7] In a large national sample, respondents were asked to say whether they thought a specified occupation had excellent, good, average, somewhat below average or poor standing, and this was to represent their personal opinion of the *general* standing that such a job had. This investigation was replicated on a smaller scale by Hodge, Siegel and Rossi in 1963.[8] As a result, prestige ratings were calculated for each occupation and it then became possible to arrange the jobs in a prestige hierarchy. The 1947 and 1963 hierarchies proved to be remarkably similar. This similarity appears to have been due in large measure to the fact that respondents were primarily influenced in their rating by pay and educational level required, and as the differential based on these two components had changed relatively little over the period 1947–63, the prestige ranking had not altered much either.[9]

The fact that the occupational prestige ranking had changed little in the United States over the stated period, and that rather similar patterns have emerged from studies in a number of other countries, should not dissuade us from looking with a critical eye at the value and significance of scales of this type. Among the doubts that arise the following may be mentioned. First there is the question of the extent of general consensus involved. There is evidence that the relative social honour attributed to two professions, for example, by respondents at different ends of the social hierarchy, may vary considerably. Thus in Britain respondents who were themselves manual workers have accorded much higher social status to a surgeon than to a stockbroker, whereas respondents who were themselves professional men have tended to give these two roughly equal status. A second difficulty concerns the grouping to be adopted, for it is one thing to obtain a rank order, and another to combine adjacent ranks into a meaningful set or hierarchy of groups. The problem here, as in so many other cases, is to find any criterion for the validation of one set of groups as compared with another. The same can be said, of course, when we attempt to do the corresponding exercise in respect of the other two variables we have been looking at, namely income/wealth and power. Once you move away from a Marxian-type dichotomy where the criteria for placement in a class are clearcut, the groupings are bound to take on a highly arbitrary appearance. One or two possible criteria are, however, worth looking at more closely.

Perhaps the most widely used distinguishing mark between types of job is the manual/non-manual dichotomy. Superficially, there is little difficulty in assigning jobs to one or other of these two categories. Convention dictates that the violinist or pianist, despite the extent to which manual dexterity may be involved in his case, is to be treated as a non-manual worker. Yet though for broad purposes it may be useful to divide a population into these two categories, there remains considerable doubt about the significance of having done so. It is not at all clear, for example, whether a manual worker either in Britain or the United States who gives up his job and takes a worse paid white-collar one instead, really feels that he has bettered himself in some status sense or not, nor do we know how his friends would evaluate the position. A second type of dichotomy involves working for oneself as against working for someone else. Here at least we do know that when someone deliberately ceases to be an employee and becomes self-employed he almost invariably claims to have bettered his position, though there is again uncertainty about the view that might be taken by others. Has he for instance sacrificed security for independence, and how are these two factors to be assessed in status terms? And would an architect or lawyer who gave up his private practice to work wholly for a public authority be regarded as having fallen in status as a consequence? In this last case the distinction at least has the virtue of being basically a Marxian one.

This last example leads us to a third possible difference in kind between occupations which has particular relevance to a status discussion, namely that between professional and other jobs. No one can be in any doubt in either of these two societies that the members of many occupations loosely described as quasi- or semi-professions show a desperate anxiety to acquire professional status, and attempt to exert great pressure on governments and to influence public opinion to this end. It can, of course, be argued that what they are really after are the better material rewards and the greater control over the qualifications of practitioners, and over the flow of entrants into the occupation, which the legal granting of such status commonly brings. To say this, however, is merely to be reminded again of the fact that the economic and power elements undoubtedly form a very large component of any status situation.

However useful they may be for particular purposes, therefore, it does not look as though any of the possible criteria for distinguishing between different kinds of occupation—manual/non-manual, employee/self-employed, non-professional/professional—can really provide an entirely satisfactory basis on which to differentiate between groups of occupations in a hierarchy. So the most we can do is to conclude that the status groupings used in, say, Lloyd Warner's community studies, and the occupational status groupings employed in national British and American studies, cannot be regarded as being more than a convenient way of simplifying what would otherwise be an unmanageable set of minute gradations, but as having no special significance beyond this. Thus to take a British example, no one should be under any delusion that the particular way of organising occupations into five Social Class Groups adopted by the Registrar General for England and Wales at the time of the 1981 population census has any greater validity than the significantly different allocation of categories bearing the same name made by his predecessors in 1971, 1961, 1951 or 1931.

STATUS-LOWERING AND STATUS-RAISING PERSONAL ATTRIBUTES

No one can reasonably doubt that in societies of the types we are considering, occupation is the major determinant of personal status. There is nothing surprising about this, for differences in skill, in responsibility, in authority and power over others, in level of education, in income and in lifestyles, arise directly from, or are closely linked with, occupation and position within that occupation, and these differences are bound to play a main part in deciding how people react to one another in social situations in deference terms. A main part does not necessarily mean the only part. Even when a person's income/wealth and occupation/position have provided the general key to the deference he is likely to be shown in the course of social interaction, he may in fact receive rather more or rather less than would be expected in his given circumstances because of other personal characteristics which are likely to have an independent influence on the situation.

Most observers of the British or American scene would probably be in broad agreement regarding the likelihood that certain personal attributes would have status-raising or status-lowering consequences. In what follows all we are really saying is that, *other things being equal*, a person's status will tend to be raised or lowered from the level dictated by economic, occupational and level of education factors, if he possesses or does not possess certain other attributes as well.

(*a*) Lineage, as the Lloyd Warner studies showed, was significant in the top levels of status attribution in small American communities. It is hardly necessary to remind ourselves of its importance in *English* society.

(*b*) Titles are also significant, in the sense of the 'right' to be addressed in a distinctive way or to add some letters after one's name, however that 'right' has been acquired.

(*c*) Modes of speech and dress cannot be denied a certain relevance in this context.

(*d*) Certain forms of 'conspicuous consumption', to use Veblen's term, can have a noticeable effect when status is being evaluated, as can indulgence in particular leisure pursuits.

(*e*) A special social status attaches to particular educational establishments. Thus, in England having been at an independent secondary school rather than one financed by the local education authority, or having been at an Oxford or Cambridge college rather than one of the other universities, tends to have status-raising effects; and there are corresponding examples to be found in the United States.

(*f*) In the case of religious affiliation, membership of the Church of England as against all other denominations is significant. And there is no need to be reminded of the independent influence of the Protestant/Catholic dichotomy in Ulster.

There remain two types of personal attribute where a certain measure of inequality of civil/legal/political rights either exists or is believed by some people to exist, in addition to the status inequality with which alone we are concerned in the present chapter.

(*g*) In both societies, certain types of ethnic origin can clearly have a bearing not merely on one's access to educational and career opportunities but also, and this is the relevant point here, on one's status, independent of occupational position actually held.

(*h*) Sex, civil status, and age are clearly pertinent as well. To be a woman rather than a man, to be a single rather than a married woman, to be too young or too old, may in both of these two societies have status-lowering consequences *in certain circumstances.*

Finally, there are two general issues to which attention can be drawn. In the first place, the independent weight to be given to status elements very much depends on the view taken regarding the degree of consensus that actually exists in status attribution. We know remarkably little about the changes that may be taking place. For instance, are the views of the younger generation on some of these matters very different from those of their elders, as is widely supposed? And does this mean that the importance attached to deference in interpersonal relations is suffering a secular decline, or is it merely that the characteristics leading to deferential behaviour or its opposite have changed? And apart from our lack of information about how the position may be changing, we are surprisingly ill-informed as to how status judgements currently operate, or used until recently to operate, in modifying interpersonal behaviour in different types of situation in everyday life in either of our two societies.

If the existence of what has been called an 'evaluation consensus' regarding the structure of status and deference can no longer be assumed, certain consequences that may not be obvious at first sight will tend to follow. One of these is that a dominant group will no longer in the same way as formerly be able to bring a deviant minority to heel by invoking the disapprobation of the majority. Or, to take an even more homely illustration, to the extent that there ceases to be general agreement on the deference due to those on whom honours have been bestowed on an English royal occasion such as the Queen's Birthday, the dominant group will have been deprived of a useful means of obtaining the compliance of potential deviant leaders.

Secondly, there is the question of 'status anxiety'. This, it has sometimes been suggested, may affect not merely individuals but whole categories of people. Where the latter occurs, and where the anxiety is more than just temporary in character, it is arguable that the political consequences can be far-reaching. Ethnic and religious groups who feel that their former privileged status is being eroded by civil rights concessions to their rivals (for example, 'poor whites', or in the Ulster setting, Protestant manual workers) can form the backbone of extremist political movements. The difficulty is to assess how much of their corpus of real and imagined grievances is to be attributed to economic, power and status anxieties respectively.

How many dimensions and how are they interrelated? 8

So far we have discussed certain groups of respects in which what might loosely be called 'structured inequality' can be seen to exist, and have distinguished economic, power and status respects. These groupings as we have employed them clearly do not exhaust the possible dimensions that have a claim to be regarded as important. What about unequal life expectancy, for example? Is this not just as basic as any of the forms of inequality we have so far considered? And what about inequality of access to educational and career opportunities (sometimes called life chances)?

Leaving these on one side for the moment, we can see that the fact of the various forms being closely interrelated makes it difficult to justify treating some as causes of the others, unless we draw an apparently arbitrary line around, say, the economic inequalities and treat all other respects in which people are socially unequal as deriving from their relative income/wealth; but empirical evidence about individuals does not confirm that this is always and necessarily the case. Great riches may represent great *purchasing* power, but others may have greater power of certain kinds than do millionaires, and greater prestige as well. Or should we, in Marxian terms, treat ownership/non-ownership of the means of production as the basic dichotomy from which all other social inequalities inevitably follow? Perhaps only by adopting a strictly Marxian approach can a logically consistent treatment be arrived at. For once we admit that there can be a number of dimensions of social inequality of which none necessarily has primacy over the others, more and more respects in which people can be seen to be unequal begin to seem worthy of inclusion as further dimensions.

Before we go on to discuss some of these other forms of inequality, however, there are two other important issues to be dealt with. The first, which can now be examined, concerns the extent to which there seems to be consistency or lack of it in the rank order of individuals on various dimensions of social inequality. This naturally leads to a discussion of how far we need to concern ourselves with more than one dimension of inequality when principles rather than matters of detail are under consideration. A second issue, discussion of which will be postponed until a later chapter, relates to the varying constructions of social reality by different individuals and groups.

In the general tradition of Weber's concern to study how far, why and with what consequences a person's ranking in economic and status terms might differ, Lenski has taken a preliminary look at some aspects of this problem, which we might call rank-order consistency.[1] He takes financial, occupational, educational and ethnic dimensions, and hypothesises that someone whose ranking is high in some of these cases but low in others will tend to experience considerable stress in interpersonal relations.[2] The basic reason why this is likely to be so is that whilst *he* will think of himself in terms of the *best* of his ratings, and will expect others to do the same, *they* are in fact likely to have an interest in doing just the opposite, by thinking of him in terms of his lowest rating. The person suffering from rank-order inconsistency could, for instance, be a Negro doctor; interacting with a white labourer in an American setting he might well not be accorded the deference he felt to be due to him. The societal importance of issues involving stress for the individual might, of course, arise in a variety of ways, for example, through such people providing the leadership for radical movements.

A related issue of very considerable importance is how far the general pattern of inequality in a given society on one dimension so closely resembles the pattern on other dimensions that it is legitimate to use one of them as representing the combined situation.

Runciman, while not denying that there are links between the three dimensions of stratification (class, power and status), claims that the usefulness of this three-dimensional approach concept can only be challenged by showing 'that any statement about economic class entails some statement about either status or power' and so on.[3] Ingham points out that Runciman has defined class and status in such a narrow way (wealth and prestige, that is, as attributes of individuals) that his challenge probably cannot be met. If, however, one redefines these terms in the more usual way so as to include also a type of *social relationship*, then the challenge can at least partially be taken up. For in that case certain, but not all, statements about class (involving an unequal market situation) are also statements about economic power relationships; certain, but not all, statements about status (involving a deference relationship) are also statements about normative power, and so on.[4] If we accept the Ingham argument, the very definition of the three dimensions in the traditional manner, implies certain logical links between them.

Parkin seems to go rather further than Ingham on the road towards accepting that there is a built-in dovetailing of class, status and power. He regards the multidimensional model, in which each individual occupies a certain rank in a variety of separate dimensions such as occupation, income and ethnic status, as possibly applicable to a limited extent to the United States but much less so to Britain and Europe. He prefers what is in effect a unidimensional approach in which the backbone of the reward system of societies of the British type is seen as an income and fringe-benefit hierarchy of broad occupational categories. The key to the particular pattern this reward structure takes in any western capitalist society at any point in time is, he says, the factor of marketable expertise scarcity.

In justifying his view that the market has in effect imposed a unitary reward system on society, he claims that other possible dimensions can be satisfactorily encompassed in this single one. Take, for instance, the dimension of property, and income from property. In his opinion this has become merged with the occupational order by developments such as business managers and professionally skilled people acquiring shareholdings, and those born to wealth becoming gainfully employed. Again, turning to the question of status, Parkin argues that, if we confine our attention to status attaching to *positions* rather than persons (and this is a very important proviso), then the principles behind the status order will be basically the same as those on which the reward structure is arrived at; for if the status order reflected some different principle, the dominant group's dominance would be endangered. Therefore the two dimensions cannot, as it were, be in conflict, and separate account need not be taken of the status dimension.[5]

If, as we hope, this is a fair summary of the Parkin argument on that particular point, we should perhaps look at some of the issues involved a little more closely before deciding how convincing it is. First of all, we have already explained that, in Parkin's view, the basic principle underlying the reward structure is scarcity of marketable skills. How far is it true to say that this same principle is the basic determinant of the relative status accorded to different offices? One difficulty here is that this intangible status element sometimes seems merely to reflect the economic factor (as when people, on being told that a particular office commands very high rewards but knowing little else about it, give it high status ranking), but on other occasions (as when badly paid jobs nevertheless command considerable prestige) seems designed to *compensate* for some economic inadequacy.

In this latter case, are we justified in saying that the principle involved is still scarcity of marketable skills? The scarcity and skill factors are certainly at work, for the positions that readily come to mind in this context usually need a high level of education and training. But what about the 'marketable' factor, since by definition these offices command relatively low pay? The answer would seem to be that high status (along with good holidays and other fringe benefits) has to be regarded as society's (that is, past and present dominant groups') way of ensuring that these positions are filled by suitably trained incumbents, and that when one talks of the 'reward structure' of society these status elements have to be considered as forming a necessary part of that structure. Viewed in this light, the status dimension, always provided we are dealing with offices and not with persons, ceases to be of independent significance, and falls into place as part of a wider strategy of which the central feature is an occupational hierarchy structured in economic terms.

In the same way, power does not, in Parkin's view, need to be regarded as a separate dimension of social stratification (provided we are looking at things at a *societal* level), for the power dimension is merely 'another way of conceptualising the distribution of class and status advantages'.[6]

Though there is a lot to be said for the Parkin view we have just outlined, it nevertheless remains true that, for example, the broad pattern of inequality in personal wealth in Britain looks substantially different from that of inequality of personal incomes (and the latter, of course, takes a very different shape before tax from that shown after tax). Wealth is much more inequitably distributed than income in either sense. If we take Parkin's 'reward structure' as consisting basically of incomes and fringe benefits resulting from occupational division of labour, one would expect this to show a similar contrast with the frequency distribution of wealth, in the sense that large personal incomes are much less concentrated in the hands of a small group of people than are large holdings of personal wealth. Obviously, however, the same people must quite often appear in the same category, high or low, of income as of wealth. And if we are dealing in terms of very broad issues indeed, it is perhaps justifiable to regard the occupational reward structure as 'representing' social inequality as a whole in a society such as Britain, and as itself being largely the product of market forces (however 'unfree' that market may be in important respects). And Parkin himself concedes that where religious or ethnic attributes carry considerable weight (for example in Ulster), it would be misleading not to take account of their influence on social inequality.

Inequality of life expectancy 9

One of the simplest ways to refute the statement often made about Britain and the United States to the effect that 'class no longer matters' is to show that class in these two societies still materially influences a person's chances of staying alive. Or to put it slightly more correctly, mortality rates continue to vary inversely with socio-economic class, and they have done so throughout the half-century during which the relevant data have been systematically collected and analysed.

To prove the point we may look first at *general* mortality. Everyone knows that one's expectation of life at birth, that is, the average future lifetime one could expect to have if subjected throughout it to the age and sex death rates of the period at which one was born, has increased. To take the England and Wales case, the figure for men has moved from forty at the middle of the nineteenth century to sixty-nine and a half in 1974–75, and for women over the same period from forty-two to over seventy-five and a half. Within this very large overall increase in expectation of life at birth (or decline in general mortality) there has, however, persisted a substantial and perhaps increasing social-class gradient. This may be shown for working-life mortality by using official figures in which the Registrar General for England and Wales has 'married' data relating to his five Social Class Groups derived from occupational information obtained at a decennial population census, with annual death registration data of roughly similar date. In order to eliminate the unwanted variable of the differing age structure of various groupings within the population, Standardised Mortality Ratios (SMRs) are calculated, a ratio of 100 being the average for the whole population at the given date, and figures higher or lower than that representing worse or better mortality experience than the average. Taking males aged twenty to sixty-four, the SMRs for the Social Class Groups were, in 1930–32, 90 for Class I (higher administrative and professional occupations and business directorships), 94 for Class II (other administrative, professional and managerial, together with shopkeepers), 97 for Class III (clerical workers, shop assistants, skilled manual), 102 for Class IV (semiskilled manual), and 111 for Class V (unskilled manual). When the same calculations were made around the time of the 1951 census, the first figures issued for the five Social Class Groups in order were 98, 86, 101, 94 and 118. This seemed to represent a major and highly favourable change in the situation as compared with the prewar period. The *Manchester Guardian* presented it as front page news under the heading 'Mortality Amended'. For the first time in England's history it seemed as though a man's expectation of life was no longer inseparably linked with his social position. Those in Class II appeared to have a more favourable mortality experience than their fellows in higher status occupations, and the semiskilled manual workers of Class IV also appeared to be more favourably situated in mortality terms than those in Class I (not to mention those in the Class immediately above them). The so-called W-effect represented by this startling series of figures was widely discussed. And though the Registrar General reminded us that the findings were not conclusive, it was natural that explanations of the new situation should abound. Not unexpectedly, in these 'lay' explanations two features tended to predominate. First, there was great emphasis on the special risks to which those in posts of high responsibility in business and elsewhere were supposed to be peculiarly prone, and much was made of ulcers and heart disease. Secondly, the apparently highly favourable situation of semiskilled manual workers was held to demonstrate the benefits already accruing from postwar improvements in standards of life and social and health facilities, notably the infant National Health Service.

Rejoicing over the apparent replacement of the social class

gradient in general mortality by the W-effect proved, however, to have been premature. For in the course of time, when fuller information became available and a closer look had been taken at the position both by those in the General Register Office and outside it, several potentially misleading aspects of these ratios came to light. First, changes in the allocation of occupations to Social Class Groups between the 1931 and the 1951 Census shifted over half a million men *out* of Class IV and an even larger number *into* it; and it so happened that the occupations involved in this transfer differed in their mortality experience. When adjustment was made for this, the apparently peculiarly favourable mortality experience of Class IV disappeared. Secondly, the different way in which the category of company directors was treated for census purposes and at death registration respectively, had a lot to do with the apparently favourable mortality experience of Class II by comparison with Class I, and when adjustment was made this peculiarity also vanished. *Official* corrected figures (for 1949–53) were not published until December 1971, and they showed that the W-effect had emerged because of errors of the type described, and the true position was again a social class gradient of the traditional type, namely 86, 92, 101, 104 and 118. At the same time the corresponding SMRs for 1959–63 were published, and these showed an even steeper gradient than either the corrected 1949–53 or the 1930–32 ones, namely 78, 81, 100, 103 and 143. Though, on the evidence of these two post-war sets of ratios, some blurring of the gradient as between Class III and Class IV (and to a lesser extent between Class I and Class II) might have taken place, the contrast between the top and bottom of the social hierarchy in respect of their general mortality seemed to have become even more striking than it was before.[1]

It is of some interest to note that when Lilian Guralnick worked out a set of SMRs for United States males aged twenty to sixty-four in 1950, for social class categories as nearly similar as possible to those used by the Registrar General in England and Wales, the ratios proved to be 83, 84, 96, 97 and 120, a gradient bearing a certain resemblance to that of the revised England and Wales ratios for 1949–53, though these revisions were not available to her and she was comparing her figures with the *uncorrected* ones showing the W-effect (as was Antonovsky in the paper reprinted in C. S. Heller, *Structured Social Inequality*, Toronto, Macmillan, 1969). The same blurring of the gradient as between Class I and Class II, and also between Class III and Class IV is noticeable.

Returning to the latest England and Wales situation, the time-lag in publishing Standardised Mortality Ratios linked with the 1971 Census was fortunately rather smaller than it had been for the 1961 Census, and they duly appeared in February 1978. For 1970–72 the social class gradient for males aged aged 16–64 proved to be almost as steep as before (77, 81, 99/106, 114, 137). Indeed, when ratios were calculated for the seventeen socio-economic groups, the experience of self-employed professional workers (69) provided an even more striking contrast with that of unskilled manual workers at the other end of the social scale (139).[2]

In due course ratios for 1980–82 will no doubt be published and we shall be able to judge whether the social class gradient in working-age mortality has flattened out at all in the decade 1971–81.

We can turn now from the differential mortality of working-age males in different social class groups to the same type of differential mortality of children before reaching their first birthdays. In England and Wales this infant mortality rate (per thousand related live births), despite showing a very encouraging overall downward trend from around 150 at the beginning of the present century to just over eleven in 1981 (associated particularly with advancing medical knowledge and its practical application, and greatly improved midwifery services) has always shown a very pronounced social class gradient, the rate in the late 1970s being twice as great in Class V as in Class I.

As to the reasons why the chances of surviving the first year of life should have varied with social origin, Douglas, in following up a national sample of children born in the first week of March 1946, found that higher infant mortality at the lower end of the social scale was partly due to the higher incidence of premature births, which in its turn was associated with early childbearing, closely spaced births, poor antenatal care, and excessive work (at home or factory) during the last months of pregnancy.[3] He also found greater mortality in the postneonatal period (from four weeks to twelve months after birth) due to greater risk of death from infections such as bronchitis, pneumonia and gastro-enteritis, which in turn was associated with more crowded living conditions and larger families. He showed how, though the children of all social classes might expect to contract at least some of the typical infections of childhood at some time, those in over-crowded homes with several brothers and sisters were more likely to contract them early in life when the risk of their being fatal was greatest. Since the early 1970s, incidentally, it has been the fall in the overall neonatal (birth to four weeks) mortality rate that has contributed most to the continued fall in infant mortality, the postneonatal rate having remained virtually unchanged. It should be noted that all the indices of infant mortality—perinatal (still-births and deaths in the first week of the baby's life), neonatal and postneonatal—show a higher incidence of death at the bottom than at the top of the social scale. This is not, of course, a feature peculiar to Britain. Thus, for example, when a comprehensive international comparative study of social and biological effects on perinatal mortality (in which eight countries participated) was organised by the World Health Organisation in the 1970s, a general tendency towards an increase in perinatal mortality rates with decrease in socio-economic status was clearly apparent in all the participating countries.[4]

In explaining the persistence of this social class gradient it has often been suggested that there is an inevitable tendency for improvements (in child-rearing as in other fields) to be adopted sooner by those higher in the social scale, and only to be taken up by those at the bottom after a considerable lapse of time. To the extent that this is valid it would imply that, even when the grosser forms of poverty have been finally eliminated, 'cultural lag' will still operate to preserve some differences in the mortality risks to which infants in the different social classes are exposed.

Finally, the current (1970–72) England and Wales data we have discussed in this chapter can conveniently be brought together in one statement spanning the bulk of a person's life, by saying that a boy's average expectation of life at birth is about seven years longer if he is subject to the mortality experience of Class I rather than to that of Class V; while if he has already survived to age 15, his remaining life expectation is 3¾ years longer in Class I than it would be in Class V.[5]

A useful summary of a 1980 report by a DHSS committee chaired by Sir Douglas Black is contained in a 1982 Penguin, P. Townsend and N. Davidson, *Inequalities in Health.*

...equality of access to educational and career opportunities 10

This chapter is about a rather different kind of inequality from those we have been considering so far, namely inequality of opportunity. Whereas the respects already dealt with in which people or families are seen to be unequal are, as it were, part of the current scene, the *opportunity* aspect in some sense underlies, precedes, and is partially responsible for, many of these other types of inequality. And there are two kinds of unequal opportunity to which we must devote attention, (*a*) inequality of access to, or opportunities to benefit from the scarcer types of secondary and higher education, and (*b*) inequality of access to higher status occupations, and to elite positions within such occupations. The second type of uneven distribution of opportunity arises partly, but by no means wholly, from the first type.

EDUCATIONAL OPPORTUNITIES

To take the first type of inequality of opportunity, it must be explained at the outset that a great deal of research has been done in this area on both sides of the Atlantic. So far as the preschool, primary and secondary aspects are concerned, we have tried to summarise this work in another book.[1] There is no room for doubt that such inequalities are still of major significance both in the United Kingdom and in the United States, and that compensatory intervention and other remedial measures are still only scratching the surface of the problem, if indeed they can really make any contribution towards solving it at all.

The main factors that can be shown to be responsible for these inequalities may be briefly indicated. To begin with, family and neighbourhood patterns of living vary very considerably from one social milieu to another, and it can be shown fairly conclusively that many features of the patterns typically found in working class urban settings, fit the child less well in terms of being able to benefit from what formal schooling provides, than do the patterns prevalent in white-collar environments. Among other related factors tending to have some bearing on the position, material poverty, poverty of experience, and family size and structure may also be mentioned. Some would argue, and with considerable justification, that in these circumstances the schools have an obligation to alter their programmes and the assumptions on which they work, so as to build upon what children from lower socio-economic levels bring with them to school. As things stand at present, however, progress made on this front has been limited and the children concerned are at a very definite disadvantage in the school setting. Their relative failure to adapt and to learn the basic skills produces for many of them what has been called a cumulative deficit in scholastic development, and they tend to fall further and further behind as their school careers continue.

One outstanding respect in which schools on both sides of the Atlantic have failed to change themselves to meet the needs of pupils from the lower half of the social hierarchy concerns the policy of testing for potential academic ability. It has been known for a very long time that the methods by which 'intelligence' is currently measured tend very much to understate the potential of such children by comparison with their middle-class counterparts, and that the situation in regard to ethnic minority children is even more unjust. Yet these tests are still very widely used at many different stages of schooling, and form one basis for teacher expectation and school policy. Teacher expectations have indeed been shown to be far too often influenced by the social background and general behaviour of the pupil, and these expectations tend to be, as everyone knows, internalised by children who then proceed to live up to or down to what the teachers expect of them. (This point is developed further in chapter 12.)

In the case of England and Wales, two characteristic features of schooling have been generally held to have widened the disparity in the relative treatment of children from differing social backgrounds. The first of these is the policy of 'streaming', whereby in many primary and secondary schools classes have been formed consisting of those within a particular range of measured ability. In practice it is known that allocation to a stream is influenced by social factors as well; and it has been clearly shown that of two children of approximately the same measured ability who find themselves in different streams, the one allocated to the higher stream tends to show progress in subsequent development and the other to show deterioration. A second feature of the educational system, the policy of selective secondary education, whereby a virtually irrevocable decision as to who should have places in the limited number of schools providing high level courses, has also been rightly credited with imposing barriers to the scholastic and occupational chances of many working-class children. And although the spread of comprehensive education (by 1982 around 83 per cent of the pupils in maintained secondary schools were in establishments run on comprehensive lines) may not have succeeded in reducing social inequalities and differences to the extent that some of the earlier reformers hoped, the opportunity structure has certainly been favourably modified thereby.

So far as the preschool, primary and secondary situation is concerned, therefore, the general picture that has been created from the wide-ranging investigations in these two countries is that of formal educational arrangements which either tend to reinforce and accentuate the relative disadvantages from which children in the lower socio-economic groups are already suffering or else are powerless to modify them substantially, however much some teachers and some education authorities might hope to do so. Put very shortly and crudely, the wider society tends to have its way. Small wonder, then, that the so-called 'de-schoolers' have in recent years attacked the whole concept of compulsory education for all children between early childhood and adolescence. Though their criticisms of what currently exists carry a good deal of weight, however, their practical proposals as to what to put in its place tend to be vague and ill-thought-out, and there are considerable doubts as to whether the relative situation of those at present disadvantaged might not be materially worsened by what they have in mind.

We may turn now to the *higher education* aspect. Here, despite large increases in the number of places made available until recently, there remain very substantial inequalities as between socio-economic groups in opportunities of access. There are a number of fairly obvious points about higher education provision of which we ought to remind ourselves at the outset. First, in all societies (including the United Kingdom and the United States) places in establishments providing some form of higher education are small in number by comparison with the age group for which they mainly cater. In these circumstances, it is a built-in feature of the social system that not every young man or young woman who may want to have such education can in fact obtain it. Secondly, whatever the precise types of evidence of previous educational attainment required before one becomes eligible for such a place, successful completion of a full course of secondary education tends in practice to be a minimum prerequisite. Thirdly, access to many forms of high status employment is made difficult if not impossible if one has failed to complete the appropriate course of higher education.

Bearing these points in mind, and particularly the second one, it becomes clear that a rough guide to inequality of access to higher education opportunities can be provided by looking at the extent of dropping out of the educational system at a stage before eligibility for higher education entry has in effect been secured. In the case of the United States we know that, for every 1,000 pupils in the fifth grade in 1928–29, 432 subsequently reached the twelfth grade, and 378 became high school graduates in 1936. We also know that twenty years later, for every 1,000 pupils in the fifth grade in 1948–49, 619 reached the twelfth grade, and 581 became high school graduates in 1956. Substantial progress had clearly, therefore, been made in that twenty-year period in the proportion of young people who were in some sense ready for higher education. Though a greater percentage of children survived to this educational stage, however, this figure inevitably concealed very large differences indeed in the survival rate of those with different types of social background. This was, of course, particularly marked in the case of ethnic minorities. Thus, only a little over half the Negroes aged twenty to twenty-nine in 1966 had completed four years or more of high school as against nearly three-quarters of their white counterparts.

Although it is difficult to make valid comparisons, if we take the nearest age cohort of English children to the bulk of the American fifth-graders of 1948–49, namely those born in the late 1930s, it has been estimated that only some 23 per cent of them entered maintained and direct grant secondary grammar schools and independent schools providing a similar type of education.[2] The remaining 77 per cent were, it is true, receiving a secondary education, but one which effectively cut them off from any likelihood of entry to full-time post-school education of most kinds. The proportion still studying at these schools at the age of seventeen had fallen to between 10 and 11 per cent of the original age cohort. It is clear, then, that at that time the American educational system was a great deal more successful than the English one in terms of the proportion of the child population brought to a secondary educational level suitable for benefiting from further full-time study. As in the case of America, the educational survival rate of children from the upper reaches of the social hierarchy was very much greater than that of children from lower down the social scale. And although there has been a marked improvement in the overall tendency to stay on at school and obtain school-leaving qualifications, it has remained true that within this overall improvement a social class gradient still operates.

In both societies, therefore, and despite the substantial differences between them in the ways in which access to higher education is provided, it can be said that a significant proportion of young people fail to succeed sufficiently in their secondary education to fit themselves for higher education, and that those who fail in this way are heavily concentrated at the lower end of the social scale. Superimposed on this is the failure for a whole variety of reasons of many of those who might be acceptable for, and might benefit from higher education, to seek such openings; and in this connection a sex differential becomes noticeable as well. All this adds up to a considerable degree of social inequality in access to higher education in both societies, though this inequality is substantially more marked in England than it is in the United States. Already, therefore, by the time the question of possible access to high status occupations requiring proof of completion of courses of higher education is reached, the population of the survivors looks very different in its social origin composition from that of survivors at earlier stages of the educational process.

CAREER OPPORTUNITIES

We must now turn to inequality of access to higher status occupations, and to elite positions within such occupations. Difficulties in designing adequate studies of recruitment to strategic elites have already been discussed in chapter 6. Though our knowledge in this field is inevitably a good deal more sketchy than in the previous one, it is clear that access to high status occupations and to elite positions within them is also very unevenly spread among socio-economic groups, even where level of previous education and standard of educational performance are kept constant. A recent United Kingdom study for which there is no close American counterpart followed up six years later a national sample of some 10,000 men and women who graduated from British universities in 1960, and was able to throw light on the differential propensity of those with varying types of social background to 'choose' (if 'choose' is the right word) from the range of types of occupation technically open to them.[3] It emerged that, even when subject studied, level of performance and type of university attended were kept constant, graduate men or women from manual-working backgrounds showed a propensity to have lower aspirations in terms of the relative status of the occupations they sought, and also actually to have entered occupations tending to be of lower status, than their counterparts with white-collar backgrounds. Contrary to what had been widely assumed, therefore, it was not true that those of humble origin who survived to this late stage of successful completion of a course of university study would no longer be handicapped by their social backgrounds. For the lower aspirational levels they had internalised, by comparison with their middle-class peers, still apparently had the effect of maintaining a measure of social inequality, this time in the form of partly self-inflicted poorer chances of access to the highest status occupations.

The whole question of how socially equal or unequal access to highly regarded occupations in a particular society actually is, becomes difficult to answer when we remember the wide range of possible situations that can exist in individual professions. Is access, for instance, restricted to university graduates or those with other higher education qualifications, or is there a variety of possible routes of entry (and, if so, what are they)? Is there an examination qualifying for entrance, and if so what is its nature? What are the constituent features of the ideal practitioner as seen by those who originally formulated, or who now operate, the profession's entry policy? Detailed study of what each profession's entry policy is, and how it operates in practice, would be needed before even the outlines of a general picture could be drawn. And an equally detailed examination of how each occupational elite compared, in social and educational background, with the population of junior recruits would also be needed (as we saw in an earlier chapter) before an attempt could be made to assess the degree of equality or inequality of access to key positions. If, in the absence of such detailed studies, a very tentative generalisation has to be made about the United Kingdom position, it would have to be that the proportion of those of humble social origin tends to be lower (*a*) the higher the positions that are being studied within a given occupation, and (*b*) the higher the status of the occupation in question by comparison with others.

Inequality of access to housing 11

A major 'new' dimension of social inequality was brought into serious discussion in 1967 when two British sociologists, Rex and Moore, published *Race, Community and Conflict*[1], namely the dimension of unequal access to housing. In the contemporary British urban context the demand for house room greatly exceeds the supply, and the resulting highly competitive situation has within it many potentialities of conflict. The opportunity to compete effectively is very unequally distributed as between different ethnic and socio-economic groups, and immigrants are particularly badly placed in this regard. They come low on the list of those eligible for council housing, and may only be offered inferior accommodation of this kind if indeed they are offered any at all. Mortgages are, for them, especially hard to obtain. As a result of these and many other constraints, the range of types of accommodation for which they are able to compete is exceptionally narrow. Within this narrow range they are unjustifiably blamed both for creating a housing shortage (which of course existed before they arrived), and for causing a deterioration in neighbourhood standards as well as in property values. Being blamed in this way stems partly from racial prejudice but has a self-fulfilling tendency to exacerbate the position.

Conditions of this kind are most often found in that one of the five concentric zones (largely arising from competition for land use) identified by Park, Burgess and McKenzie as the zone of transition.[2] In their formulation, this area resulted from the expansion of the Central Business District rendering the adjacent locations undesirable for residential purposes and only fit for transients. In Britain such a zone often involves changes in building occupancy and character of *building* use rather than a change in land use. Victorian town houses fall vacant on the death of the owner, and are then bought and let off in rooms to tenants who are desperate to find accommodation of any kind. 'This happens again and again, and soon the character of the area is changed and its function shifted from that of town residence for the wealthy to that of a place of refuge for a transient population, often varied in nationality and class.'[3]

One of the novel features of the Rex and Moore study was that in their analysis of the empirical data collected in the Sparkbrook district of Birmingham, a predominantly twilight or transitional zone not highly regarded as an area in which to live, they identified a number of housing class situations. In the first instance these were five in number: (1) owner-occupiers, though most of these lived in better residential locations; (2) council tenants; (3) tenants of whole private houses; (4) lodging-house proprietors; (5) tenants of lodging-houses. At a later stage it seemed sensible to subdivide the first of these classes by distinguishing outright owners from mortgage payers, and also to subdivide council tenants into those occupying a house with a long life and those in slum property scheduled for demolition in due course. The classification thus became a sevenfold one, and a vital feature of it was that the situations represented by these classes could be said to be in order of their relative desirability as seen by members of the host society and also, deriving from that, as seen by immigrants. In short, it could be said that nearly everyone would have as their top preference that of being an outright owner-occupier, and as their least preferred situation, that of being a lodging-house tenant, with the other five possible situations in the given order between these two extremes. But though not quarrelling with this general proposition, some critics have argued that a rather different list of categories is needed, taking account of the relative status of varying possible areas for residence, as well as of the basis on which a dwelling is occupied. Thus, Barnett, Pickvance and Ward in a Manchester study used a housing classification in which the variables related to ownership (private/council), type (owner-occupied/rented), and location (inner area/intermediate area/outer suburbs).[4] Such a formulation enables the movement of a resident from a less to a more desirable residential area to be treated as a change in his housing class (which is probably how he would regard it) even though no change in type of tenure is involved.

The impression must not be conveyed that Rex and Moore attach too little importance to the location aspect of housing, even though it may not have figured sufficiently prominently in their actual scheme of housing classes. In fact the idea of zones and of constantly changing land and building use forms an important element in their argument. Urban social stratification as they see it is rightly describable as a *process* in which a game of leapfrog is being played, the aim being, as far as one's resources and other constraints will allow, to move away from areas that are becoming less desirable and into those that are becoming more so, and to change one's relationship in the accommodation scramble from that of tenant to mortgaged owner-occupier and then to outright owner.

The basic approach of Rex and Moore in the construction of their housing class model owes something to both Marx and Weber. The idea that someone's class is economically determined and arises from his ability or lack of ability to acquire property derives from Marx. On the other hand, their housing classes do not involve a simple dichotomy between those who own property and those who do not, but include a set of seven ways in which one can obtain the use of accommodation, ranging from outright property ownership at the one extreme, to a very insecure form of tenancy at the other. And this aspect of their model is very much in the Weberian tradition. Use of the term 'class' rather than 'category' has naturally led to a good deal of discussion as to how far the groupings identified by Rex and Moore really constitute what is commonly meant by classes. They stress that the housing class one finds oneself in has a lot to do with other aspects of one's life in terms of associations, interests, life styles and position in the urban social structure. It is important to realise, moreover, that the basis of their grouping involves *relationships*, and not just the attributes of individuals. In this sense their use of the term 'class' to describe those with a similar relationship to the market (in this case the housing market) is very much in the classical tradition. On the other hand, some have argued that those caught up in the same housing class may be heterogeneous in many respects other than those mentioned above (including their differing geographical location within a city). And even if one emphasises the common elements in their situation rather than the divergent ones, they are still likely to form a 'class-in-itself' rather than a 'class-of-itself' in the Marxian sense, where the additional element of class consciousness and common aims has to be present.

The specifically *race relations* aspect of the Rex and Moore argument can be briefly summarised as follows. A conflict situation is generated by the existence of the differing housing class interests, which in its turn derives from the unequal distribution of power over living accommodation. And in their Birmingham study this conflict necessarily took on a racial character, partly because the 'gatekeepers', by preventing immigrants from entering the top four housing classes, had forced them into the bottom three, partly because the newcomers then became 'scapegoats' on whom housing inadequacies could unjustly be blamed, and partly as a result of a belief system in which the immigrant, both because of his colour and his area of origin, was felt only to be entitled to colonial status at the bottom of the social hierarchy. The lodging-house proprietor, working on the basis of short-term and costly loans, had to take in as many tenants as possible, and could therefore be pictured as a 'pariah' who destroyed good houses, grossly overcrowded them, and exploited defenceless tenants; the fact that he was performing an essential service neglected by others could conveniently be ignored.

The general validity of this account is not seriously disputed, but some have doubted whether it is equally true of immigrants from *all* overseas areas that they are forced to become proprietors of lodging-houses for fellow immigrants. In a study of a particular district of Newcastle upon Tyne, for example, it was claimed that many immigrants in fact chose of their own accord to live in and own lodging houses.[5] This, it was argued, was particularly true of those from Asia, for whom the acquisition of property was a policy often pursued for reasons other than being compelled to do so by the limitations resulting from the 'discrimination process'.

It is, of course, obvious to anyone that it is not only in access to *housing* that ethnic minorities tend to be very unequally treated. The immigrants whom Rex and Moore studied were, for example, also probably in a worse position than their nearest English counterparts in access to highly regarded occupations, in their children's educational and career opportunities, and in many other respects. Is not ethnicity, therefore, to be regarded as to some extent an independent and overriding factor in the stratification system, and ought we not to be making some general statement about it (other than the very brief treatment in the chapter on status inequality)? Runciman has indicated why generalisations of this kind are in effect ruled out. 'So many relations between ethnicity and stratification are possible that we are left with virtually as many models as cases.'[6] There is, as he says, a very wide range of situations in which stratification is *to some degree* a function of race relations. How far this applies in a particular case 'will revolve around the effect of ethnicity on the nature and extent of status mobility in the society in question'.[7] This is clearly an issue of the first importance for both the societies with which we are here concerned, but it is not one on which as yet the available research evidence enables even the outlines of a reliable picture to be drawn for their ethnic minorities as a whole.

related attitudes and behaviours 12

As explained at the outset, this book is about social differences that involve inequality, in the sense that the general view in Britain and the United States would be that more income or wealth is to be preferred to less, and that the same could be said of more power, status, life expectancy, and education, career and housing-access opportunities. To attempt in addition to treat in any reasonably comprehensive fashion social differences *not* necessarily involving inequality, would require a much larger book and one of an altogether different kind. There are, however, certain class-related attitude and behaviour differences which are particularly closely linked with some of the inequalities we have discussed. A very brief treatment of a few of these can therefore be provided, more with a view to indicating the range they cover than with any intention of exploring them adequately.

VALUE ORIENTATIONS

It is generally accepted that in most societies, and certainly in those of Britain and the United States, the societal values tend to be those of the dominant group, that is, the white middle and upper classes. It is also widely accepted that important subgroups within such societies (whether ethnic minorities, socio-economic groups or local communities) tend, in their subcultures, to conform to some of the societal, dominant group values, but not to others. To the extent that this is so, it is obviously of great importance to know what are the similarities and what are the differences between the basic assumptions characteristic of each of the important subcultures and those of the dominant social group. Naturally, the basic values underpinning the educational system will also tend to be those of the dominant group. It follows, therefore, that the degree of difficulty experienced by children in conforming to the culture of the school will depend to a significant extent on the 'goodness of fit' between the basic assumptions of the subculture to which their families belong and those of the wider society (that is, the dominant group within it).

A particularly widely quoted example may be given. As a reflection of their future-time orientation, middle-class families have generally tended where appropriate to defer present gratification in the interests of greater rewards later on; and the socialisation of their children has sought to secure the internalisation of this principle. Working-class families, on the other hand, have traditionally and realistically had a present rather than a future time orientation, and the deferred gratification implication in the policies and attitudes of schools and teachers has therefore tended to be not merely unfamiliar but also unacceptable to many children whose early socialisation has taken place in a working-class setting.[1]

PATTERNS OF LIVING

The case just quoted is merely one example of important differences in the primary socialisation of children reared in different social strata. Put in its most general form, no one would deny that a child's behaviour when he first comes to school is likely to reflect, to an important extent, what he has internalised from his family and neighbourhood setting. If, therefore, there are forms of behaviour and attitudes of mind more commonly found in a slum environment than in other urban settings, and if these conflict with what the school expects, then slum children will be likely to appear deviant from the outset. As Miriam Goldberg puts it, 'the child's view of society is limited by his immediate family and neighbourhood where he sees a struggle for survival which sanctions behaviour viewed as immoral in the society at large'.[2]

A number of commonly quoted examples may be given. It is sometimes said that in the slum milieu violence is more readily resorted to than rational discussion as a means of settling differences, which is in conflict with the basis on which schools try to operate. Again, it is usually claimed that those representing outside authority (the police, teachers and so on), are looked on as enemies rather than as helpers. It is also held that children from such an environment naturally hold education itself in low regard, partly because it seems to have been lacking in the case of the adults with whom they come in contact, and partly because of a lack of interest in, or a hostility towards, education which they observe on all sides.

The whole question of child-rearing practices and their possible effects on the personality and behaviour of the children is extraordinarily complex. Fashions, both in the practices themselves, and in the interpretation of their long-term effects, change fairly frequently. Middle-class mothers have often been credited with over-strict toilet training, and this was at one time believed to lead to particular types of personality defect in their children. Similarly, working-class parents have been held to be over-indulgent to their younger children in some respects, and too harsh in others, and it has been claimed that the erratic nature of discipline in the working-class household failed to internalise in the children satisfactory guidelines for behaviour. It has also been asserted that working-class child-rearing does not inculcate expectation of reward for task completion, and that its products are therefore ill-adapted to school patterns of goals and prizes. Perhaps the only generalisation that should be made is merely to say that, in so far as child-rearing practices differ substantially in slum as against other urban environments, the children concerned *may* experience school difficulties as a result if the school (as usually happens) is working on particular assumptions linked with contemporary middle-class child-rearing arrangements.[3]

There are many other aspects of the differing life styles of, e.g., the families of labourers and of urban white-collar workers, that can have a bearing on the relative ease with which their children can benefit from formal education, and hence on their degree of inequality of educational opportunity. Some implications of differential fertility as between socio-economic groups will be discussed in a later chapter on social mobility. The overcrowded living conditions typical of those low in the social hierarchy, as we have seen, form a contributory factor in reducing life expectancy for young children; they also make homework more difficult, or even impossible, for older children. Parental attitudes towards their children's education (and towards encouraging them to borrow books from libraries) differ markedly as between the various social strata, though, as explained earlier, not in the crude form that only middle-class parents have attitudes favourable to the child's scholastic progress.

TEACHER BEHAVIOUR

A rather specialised but nevertheless very important type of class-related behaviour concerns the partly instinctive differential reaction of many school teachers to pupils from differing types of social background. One recent example may be given, based on a very interesting observational study of a group of American black children during their kindergarten and first and second elementary school years.[4] Although many previous researches had made it clear that where the teacher expected high performance she tended to receive it, and vice versa, relatively little work had been done to find out either on what basis the teacher's original differential expectations had been formed, or the ways in which they manifested themselves in the context of the classroom. It was on these two aspects of the matter that attention was focused in this study.

After close observation of what went on in the classroom it emerged, first of all, that the teacher had an image of an 'ideal pupil' in respect of the characteristics she thought a child needed in order to be successful in school and in life, and these characteristics were in the main associated with social background factors. Secondly, when she first met the children (as well as on evidence from a variety of sources about their social, but not their intellectual, features), she formed a judgement on the extent to which they did or did not possess the characteristics of her 'ideal pupil'. And on the basis of this she grouped them as those she expected to be 'fast learners' and 'slow learners' respectively. Thirdly, having grouped them in this way, she subsequently treated the two groups very differently. The 'fast learners' had a disproportionate share of her attention and professional skills; the 'slow learners' not only came off badly in these respects, but the control-oriented behaviour of the teacher towards them contrasted sharply with the rewards and encouragement she gave to the other group. Once established, these patterns quickly became so rigid as to be almost caste-like in nature. Those originally placed in the 'slow learner' group had no option but in fact to *become* slow learners, whether this had been a true assessment of their abilities or not. By the end of the year the teacher's prophecies had duly fulfilled themselves and quasi-objective evidence, in the form both of tests and of work completed, then became available to form the basis for within-classroom grouping in the next and subsequent years of the children's schooling. So what began as a classification founded on the teacher's *subjective* assessment of the children (in its turn based on evidence of almost everything except their possible intellectual potential), perpetuated itself in later schooling as an apparently (but partly spurious) *objective* assessment of their scholastic capacity. Summing the matter up, Rist concludes that 'the public school system not only mirrors the configurations of the larger society, but also significantly contributes to maintaining them'.[5]

VOTING BEHAVIOUR

It is generally accepted that in advanced capitalist societies there is an association between social class and political attitudes, and both in the United Kingdom and the United States recent empirical evidence supporting such a contention is available. It has, however, emerged quite clearly that factors other than social class also have some influence on party allegiance. If this were not the case one could expect, for example, that the British Labour Party would receive virtually all working-class votes, while middle-class voters would be equally loyal to the Conservative Party. Were these expectations to be one hundred per cent fulfilled, Britain would have a permanent Labour Government and the Conservative Party virtually no chance of ever gaining control. The existence of Conservative Governments in the recent past is, therefore, in itself evidence that party preference is not wholly tied to the social class factor, and that a significant proportion of voters do not vote on class lines. Such deviants can, of course, be found at all social levels. Among the middle and upper classes there have traditionally always been certain individuals who tried politically to improve the lot of those less fortunate than themselves. But in recent years attention has tended to be concentrated on the working-class deviants.

In Britain, McKenzie and Silver have carried out various investigations designed to assess, particularly in respect of working-class voters, how political commitment is determined.[6] Comparing the background of working-class voters in their sample who said they had voted Conservative, with those who said they had voted Labour in the 1964 election, little emerged to distinguish the two groups from each other. The main differences seemed to be that older voters, and in particular older women, tended to veer to the right, while younger people, and in particular younger women, tended to veer to the left. When the head of a household was a trade unionist there was a likelihood that the rest of the family would favour the Labour Party. And some of those in this working-class sample who voted Labour because they held orthodox Labour views on many general issues, were also found to hold fairly Conservative views on more specific issues. Manual workers who thought of themselves as middle class were more likely to vote Conservative than those who clung staunchly to traditional working-class attitudes and values. This fits, of course, with the findings of the study by Goldthorpe and others of the prosperous car workers at Luton, who showed no inclination to align themselves with Conservatives as their incomes grew larger, but continued to vote for the party they had always supported.

So far as the ideologies of these working-class deviants were concerned, McKenzie and Silver found them to be far from apathetic in their attitudes towards politics; they had no doubts about the superiority of the party they supported. Historically very many working-class supporters of the Conservative Party had deferential attitudes towards the upper classes, and held the view that intelligence and capacity for leadership were correlates of high social status. They had no feeling of themselves wanting to usurp the elite group's position; instead, their attitude was one of feeling a responsibility to support, by giving them their votes, traditional institutions, and individuals who had inherited qualities of leadership. Working-class voters who held such views were described by McKenzie and Silver as *deferentials*. Over a period of time the number of deferential working-class Conservative voters has been dwindling, this being especially true of those in the younger age groups, whilst men are less inclined to deferential attitudes than are women. McKenzie and Silver class as *seculars* the more worldly and practical of the working-class Conservatives who do not hold these deferential views. These voters base their support for Conservatism on their evaluation of the party's policies, achievements and general management of the economy. Though they may be willing to accept traditional institutions, they are nevertheless prepared and able to criticise them.

So in Britain there has been a shift in the ideological basis of working-class Conservatism from deference in the direction of secularism, and the authors note that working-class Conservatives with higher incomes are more likely to be seculars than deferentials. From all this they suggest that strong connections can be detected between income, age and sex on the one hand, and political cleavage within the working class on the other. The whole ideological basis of working-class Conservatism is shifting, and groups with deferential attitudes are likely to prove decreasingly important. At present secularism is found most strongly amongst the younger age groups, amongst the most highly paid, and amongst men.

In the United States social class appears to have less direct linkage with political attitudes than has been found in the British investigations. Steinberg and Selznick made an analysis of the 1964 Presidential election in terms of social class and party preference voting behaviour, and estimated the extent to which basic political beliefs may or may not crumble in the face of what appear to voters to be immediate social class interests.[7] In American Presidential elections the normal pattern is for the Democratic candidate to win a higher proportion of the manual workers' votes than his Republican adversary, and conversely for a higher proportion of the more prosperous middle classes to support the Republican choice. In the 1964 election, Goldwater's manifesto offered those who normally held right-wing beliefs many policies which appealed to them (eradication of socialism and communism from within the United States, tightening up of lax community morals, a brake on the ever-increasing powers of the Federal Government, and so on), but he clamped down hard on social welfare, particularly on Medicare. By contrast, Johnson's programme was heavily biased towards social welfare. In the analysis of the overwhelming defeat sustained by Goldwater it was evident that many voters who normally subscribed to fairly conservative political ideologies transferred their allegiance, at least temporarily, and cast their votes for Johnson. This was true of *all* classes, but as one might expect, it was most true of the blue-collar workers.

In the view of the researchers it was not so much a matter of voters being converted to new political beliefs of a more liberal character, but rather that economic considerations were given precedence over others when the final judgement was made. And this was as likely to happen among the privileged as among the underprivileged if they felt their purses were going to be badly affected. Many who normally subscribed to a conservative ideology were willing to abandon their beliefs when economic difficulties loomed on the horizon. Steinberg and Selznick suggest that in America today practical economic issues are generally the prime consideration, though it is, of course, true that social class background may influence the way in which people interpret the policies put before them. Where individuals are relatively uncommitted to any particular political preference, social class may be a significant variable; but with others, who hold strong and consistent political views, social class will make little difference and they will vote in accordance with their beliefs.

In both societies, then, there is some evidence to support the view that political leaders can no longer rely to the same extent as formerly on mass support on social class lines. It remains true, however, that social class still influences voting behaviour in Britain more than in most other countries, though working-class deviants are less likely to be deferentials and more likely to be seculars (and the creation of the SDP may, if they continue to win electoral support, somewhat reduce the old type of influence of social class on voting behaviour). Another major unknown factor is how the strategy of the leaders of the main parties will influence social class linkage. For although it may be in each party's interests to avoid polarisation of this kind, politicians are not immune from failure to foresee the hidden electoral consequences of their policies, and they may inadvertently bring about the very situation they are anxious to avoid.

It may be noted, finally, that a very recent major study provides evidence of a substantial erosion of traditional class support for the Labour Party in Britain during the last decade. Future analysis of the 1983 General Election will no doubt confirm these pre-election findings.[8]

Differing constructions of reality 13

We move now to an examination of a whole group of issues, only touched on so far, that many sociologists would regard as of such importance that they ought to have been discussed at length at the very outset. These issues arise from the circumstance that a man interprets his social situation in his own way, influenced both by what he has internalised in the course of his primary and secondary socialisation *and* by his own creative imaginative effort. He then proceeds to act on his particular interpretations (including his actions in the socialisation of his children). In short, his typifications, constructions and interpretations of reality are his guides to everyday action; and when these are reciprocally shared by many others, institutionalisation may be said to have taken place. Once this happens legitimation may also occur, whereby the institutions concerned are explained and justified. Subworlds or subcultures thus come to have their own systems of meaning, partly separate from and partly common to society at large[1].

To find out empirically how these social meanings vary and what significance attaches to the variations, is a task that has rarely been conscientiously undertaken. Sociologists have on the whole been content to study only *one* pattern of institutionalised typifications and to assume that this applies throughout a given society, and this is nowhere more noticeable than in the field of social stratification. Despite the obvious fact that in this field we are concerned with how men evaluate others as unequal in respects they see as being important, remarkably little work has been done to discover which inequalities are seen by different groups of people as relatively more significant than others, on what basis they assess them, and how their own social behaviour is geared to them; for example, are they led to associate with, avoid or act deferentially towards those whom they see as unequal to them in particular respects? Both the wide range of possible ways of looking at the same so-called objective fact of inequality, and our lack of knowledge regarding the frequency with which varying possible interpretations of reality are actually held, can be conveniently illustrated by taking two simple examples. First, to know that A has such-and-such an income and B has one a given amount larger, tells us little of value unless we also know the social meaning of income to both A and B and to those with whom they interact. For income may be seen in so many different ways—as a means of improving one's standing in the eyes of others, of providing material possessions for oneself or one's family, of indulging charitable feelings towards those suffering from misfortune, of obtaining power of certain types over others, and so on.

As a second example, let us suppose that a number of people chosen at random are shown a table of figures giving the distribution of wealth in Britain in the late 1970s, whereby, for instance, 1 per cent of the population owned between 24 and 13 per cent of the total wealth (depending on how it was defined), and that the randomly chosen respondents are asked for their reactions to this.

Some would react on the basis of value judgements regarding desirable or undesirable *sources* of wealth. A case of this kind would be that of an observer who had no objection to the unequal distribution of wealth provided that none of that inequality stemmed from inheritance. Or again, it might be felt that apparently passive wealth acquisition by, say, simply receiving dividends from share holding or income from renting property was objectionable, whereas wealth acquired actively by personal effort and the exercise of initiative was not. Another variant would involve discriminating between wealth acquired by what were held to be antisocial forms of enterprise (for example, the manufacture or distribution of alcoholic drinks, drugs or armaments, the provision of facilities for gambling, prostitution, pornography, criminal activities, and so on) and wealth arising from what were considered more legitimate activities. An interesting variation, where there are reasons for believing that the view is fairly widely held in our own society, relates to wealth stemming from windfalls. If the reported reactions of many people on hearing of large fortunes being acquired as a result of wins on the pools are taken at their face value ('Good luck to them'), then an uneven distribution of wealth associated solely with windfalls of this kind would not apparently arouse feelings of injustice in many people's minds, on the perhaps shaky assumption that 'it might be my turn next'. What is believed to be another widely held variant, the meritocratic view, takes the form of objecting to the unequal distribution of wealth solely to the extent that it can be shown to reflect a societal unequal distribution of opportunities to acquire wealth, in such matters as unfairness in educational arrangements and in access to highly paid occupations.

It can readily be seen, therefore, that even among those whose basic objection to the pattern of wealth distribution in their own society relates primarily to the *source* of that wealth, the political or other measures that might satisfy them are of very varying nature and the issues involved are anything but straightforward. To what, for instance, do they attribute the particular inequalities to which they take exception (specific features of the capitalist system, or mistakes of omission or commission by past governments), and what measures, political or other, do they think would now be likely to be most effective in bringing about a more acceptable situation? And one would have to take account of such factors as ignorance of available evidence or faulty interpretation of it, leading to possible wrong attribution of causes and wrong selection of appropriate remedial measures.

Then there is the question of *motivation*. Some people would argue that wealth acquired as a byproduct of activity in which one was trying to exercise one's talents to the full, or to benefit one's fellow men, or to provide the best for one's family, was on a different footing from riches associated with greed. Those who hold views of this kind occupy a position of peculiar difficulty in deciding whether they should be critical or otherwise of what is happening in their own society, since reliable information on people's motivation is almost impossible to come by. What, for example, are we to make of the well-known belief that many business tycoons continue to amass wealth long after its acquisition has ceased to interest them, more out of habit than anything else?

Closely allied to the question of the motivation of the wealth acquirers is that of the *use* to which they ultimately put their wealth. Whatever their motives in the course of becoming wealthy, there is certainly a widespread feeling that millionaires who subsequently distribute a substantial proportion of their riches in the form of charity or educational endowments, represent wealth-holding and inequality of wealth distribution in a much less objectionable form than where riches are, say, merely transmitted to descendants. Even in this category there can be complicating factors. Suppose, for example, that a successful local industrialist ploughs back part of the wealth he has acquired into greatly extending the enterprise, and so creating additional jobs for large numbers of local people. It goes without saying that in these circumstances the maldistribution of wealth represented by his past gains would be very much more tolerantly viewed by fellow citizens in that area, than if he had merely spent them in riotous living.

The extreme example of an *egalitarian* standpoint would be to take the view that any departure from absolute equality in wealth distribution between, say, adult members of a society was objectionable, and that the greater the departure the greater the objection. Even in this case, however, there is a less extreme variant. The well-known maxim 'From each according to his ability, to each according to his needs', would seem to leave some room for inequality of income, provided that inequality only reflected unequal family responsibilities or something of this sort; but what other kinds of need, if any, should one take into account? Some would accept the legitimacy of what actually exists, having internalised a belief that those in control of society's affairs know best what is in the interests of the community as a whole. Others might take a *meritocratic* stance, to the effect that there was nothing wrong with the *status quo* provided there could be shown to be no constraints on access to educational and career opportunities by those from humble social backgrounds.

Our classification would be incomplete if we did not include people who, in some fashion, accept a situation merely because it exists. Thus a man may feel that the question of the justice or injustice of a particular societal distribution of wealth is irrelevant, since in his view he can do nothing about it and he just has to live with things as they are. Such an attitude can be combined with a particular view as to how best to help one's children 'work the system'. The father who has himself been disappointed by his own lack of material success may, as we shall see, interpret what he has seen in his own working life as showing that paper qualifications are what matter most in getting on, and so endeavour to encourage or dragoon his sons into the acquisition of as many certificates as possible. Such a man may feel himself to be a realist, but this realism can be combined with a view of the society in which he lives as either being just or unjust. It is arguable that what matters in this case is not his feelings regarding the *ethics* of society, but his view of what is happening, on the basis of which he decides how best to ensure that his sons shall fare better than he did himself.

Up to this point, in our second example, we have shown how the same objective reality can be subjectively conceived in quite different and often mutually antagonistic ways by different people (or, more importantly, groups of people). In practical situations, of course, people are rarely reacting towards the *same* set of objective data, but are more usually reacting towards different scraps of data some of which may be true and some false, but which hardly ever give a reliable overall picture of what the factual situation really is. But as Hiller puts it, 'people's perception of "the truth" . . . even if it is objectively incorrect, and their reaction to "the truth" being shown to them, are social facts of at least equal importance to "the truth" itself'.[2]

Enough has probably been said to demonstrate that any attempt to categorise people in two or three groups in respect of their supposed attitudes towards the reward system of the society in which they live and work, is potentially highly misleading. For not only are the possible basic attitudes quite numerous, but there are also endless opportunities and even likelihoods of composite attitudes deriving from several bases in combination with each other. An obvious example of this would be that of someone who combines a belief that an egalitarian distribution of wealth would be the fairest system, with a belief that certain forms of wealth acquisition are nevertheless less objectionable than others. And the plain fact is that on all these issues we have almost no empirical evidence from any society on which to base generalisations about the relative frequency with which differing attitudes are in fact held, and how strongly they are held. It is, moreover, patently obvious that any attempt to discover people's attitudes on such issues will inevitably bring to light the fact that many people have given little serious thought to these matters, and may well hold views involving internal inconsistencies (for example, how it affects *me* as against what might be right for society at large). Small wonder, then, that when we seek to take account of people's differing perceptions of reality in the field of social stratification, we seem to be entering a maze of almost limitless possibilities with virtually no guide lines.

To return to the main line of argument, it hardly needs to be emphasised that what we are faced with in a society such as that of Britain or the United States is not a single system, but multiple and overlapping systems of social stratification. In the case of the British working class, Lockwood, for example, distinguishes three important subgroups with very different images of society: the traditional working class, divided into those with a proletarian and those with a deferential outlook, and the new working class with its privatised way of looking at things.[3] Taking contemporary western capitalist societies generally, and not just Britain, as his frame of reference, Parkin distinguishes three major 'meaning systems' (and four types of consequential response) as characterising the attitudes of different sections of the subordinate class towards the social inequalities in their society. First, there is the dominant value system, in conformity with the country's major social institutions, and legitimating the *status quo*. Those in the subordinate class who have internalised this particular value system, define the reward structure either in *deferential* or in *aspirational* terms. Secondly, there is the subordinate value system stemming from the local working-class community, and leading those who have internalised it to make what he calls 'accommodative' responses.[4] Though conceptualising the position in terms of 'them' and 'us', though often conscious of the basic unfairness of the reward structure, and though imbued with a strong sense of community solidarity, this kind of response falls far short of the class consciousness Marx had in mind as the necessary prelude to militant action. Trade unionism is one expression of what is basically a product of working-class life on a local level. Thirdly, and in strong contrast, is the radical value system stemming from a mass working-class political movement, and leading to an *oppositional* attitude towards the reward structure, representing class consciousness in the traditional sense.

Both Lockwood and Parkin are clearly in general agreement that there is no longer any large measure of consensus, if indeed there ever was, throughout societies of the type we are discussing, or within broad groupings in such societies, on how they see their country's pattern of social inequality, *or* what view they take on the legitimacy of the system, *or* what action (individual or collective, short-term or long-term) they feel should be taken in relation to it. The belief that either in Britain or the United States there is some broad measure of acceptance at all social levels of the dominant group ideology on social stratification, has certainly declined over the last two decades. On the contrary, it is now much more usual to accept that, in all probability, within any given community or society, people are working on the basis of significantly different sets of typifications regarding inequality as they see it, however difficult it may be to establish empirically just what these are and how widely each is held.[5] Are we, then, still justified in attaching importance to the American Creed? This was the ideology said until recently to have been internalised by many or most citizens of the United States (or at least those who were White, Anglo-Saxon and Protestant), to the effect that theirs was a society of equal opportunity, that those at the top therefore deserved to be there because of their ability, education and hard work, and those at the bottom could equally be thought of as justifiably there by virtue of lack of these characteristics. No corresponding ideology in the form of a British creed seems to have been identified. And it has never been established whether it was better for the self-esteem of the materially unsuccessful person to be able to blame the social system for his failure, or to have to lay it at the door of poor natural endowment and/or lack of industry on his own part. It is also worth noticing in passing that one complication is missing when our immediate concern is with two societies of the present type, since the use of central coercive power to produce an *artificial* consensus is fortunately ruled out: if we do find some measure of consensus, it is at least 'committed conformity' rather than merely 'overt conformity' to a system seen by certain participants as illegitimate.

Considerable difficulties arise when we try to design any programme of empirical enquiry into social stratification that will take account of people's varying constructions of reality. For ideally the questions to which responses are sought should provide information on at least three dimensions: his own personal belief, his perceived beliefs of those who (to him) are significant others, and his perceived beliefs of 'most people'. If these three dimensions are always to be covered when questioning him about any aspect of the subject, as would seem to be necessary if a meaningful picture is to emerge from the aggregation of individual responses, it can readily be seen how sophisticated and how time-consuming future field surveys will have to be, compared with those to which we have hitherto been accustomed.

At this point it might be useful to give some attention to an aspect of the matter on which a fair amount of empirical data has been collected, namely, that of self-identification (or self-rating) in stratification terms. In various national polls conducted in the United States in the 1940s, people were asked to say to which of three named social classes they felt they belonged, upper, middle or lower. Between four-fifths and nine-tenths of them placed themselves in the middle class. When Centers subsequently repeated this exercise but provided a fourth possible category, the working class, many respondents availed themselves of this new possibility and the earlier findings were clearly shown to have been heavily influenced by the particular choices offered.[6] It did not require much perspicacity to see that people would be reluctant to class themselves as 'lower', whereas 'working' conjured up a more favourable picture, and was in the tradition of the Protestant ethic. A few years later Gross finally killed the belief that any forced-choice questions on an issue of this kind could really produce useful results.[7] For when he merely asked 'What class do you belong to?', about a third of the respondents failed to identify themselves with any class at all, claiming either that they did not know where to place themselves, or that social classes did not exist, or that they themselves were outside the class system.

An English example of a more interesting use of self-identification or self-rating in stratification terms is provided by Runciman's survey where he questioned a sample of 1,087 adult men and women in 1962. He classified his respondents occupationally as manual or non-manual, and within each of these groups distinguished two subgroups according to whether they rated themselves as being working class or middle class. He found that, in terms of the income they said they had, 'manual workers and their wives are consistently less likely to feel relatively deprived than are non-manual workers and their wives who are earning the same'.[8] This was, of course, because they were comparing themselves with very different reference groups. However, even those manual workers who rated themselves as middle class did not feel significantly more deprived than fellow manual workers who rated themselves as working class.

In order to throw light on attitudes bearing on inequalities of status, Runciman asked a number of questions regarding type of education and type of job respondents would like their actual, or hypothetical, sons to have. On these issues not only did there emerge the expected differences between manual and non-manual respondents, but within the manual group those who rated themselves as middle class gave answers showing greater feelings of relative deprivation in status terms than did manual workers who assigned themselves to the working class. The important finding was, therefore, that self-assignment to the middle class had an effect on the attitudes of manual workers and their wives towards inequalities of *status* in a way that it did not have on their attitudes towards inequalities of income. It is, of course, likely that manual working respondents categorising themselves as middle class or working class were merely reflecting the same status attitudes which were again elicited when the questions about education and careers for sons were asked.

In recent years there have been increasing doubts regarding the value of asking general questions not merely on self-identification with a specified social class, but even self-rating in an open-ended form. As explained earlier in this chapter, we need to find out not merely how the respondent himself sees things, but also how he thinks people at large (*and* those who to him are significant others) see things. In the context of self-rating this would mean asking the respondent at the same time to say what class he puts himself in, what class he thinks people in general put him in, and what class he thinks those who know him personally put him in.

Putting it very shortly, we have in the past paid too much attention to the reality of social stratification as perceived by theorists on the one hand, and those conducting field surveys on the other, and far too little regard to how reality is perceived by different groups of people who come into neither of these very restricted categories. As yet we know very little about *their* conceptions of social class and social inequality, and more knowledge of this would be invaluable in understanding what is happening or is likely to happen. In gaining such knowledge we must not, however, expect to find entirely new concepts and patterns, in sharp contradiction to those we have hitherto rather arbitrarily assumed to exist, for the concept of class based on the writings of Engels and Marx, for instance, has been so much part of the common currency of political debate for so long that it is bound to have had a major influence, through the processes of primary and secondary socialisation, on the conceptions of reality of succeeding generations of adults in many walks of life. It is not so much a question, therefore, of *discarding* all that has hitherto passed for theory and objective fact, but of attempting to *validate* it by much more sophisticated efforts to find out about the constructions of reality of ordinary people which, when widely held and acted on, can claim to be just as objective, just as factual, and just as significant as the 'hard' data found in tabulations of official statistics.

Social mobility 14

When a person ascends or descends the social stratification ladder, whether within the course of a lifetime (intragenerationally) or in comparison with parental social position (intergenerationally), upward or downward social mobility can be said to have occurred. The social significance of this movement depends partly upon the distance 'travelled' and on the effects for the mobile individual of the 'journey'. But the study of social mobility has also attracted much theoretical and empirical attention because it is seen to provide important information about the characteristics of social structure and process. The nature, rates, consequences and overall significance of social mobility remain, nevertheless, subjects of active debate.

SOCIETAL IMPLICATIONS OF HIGH AND LOW MOBILITY RATES

The most commonly-encountered view claims social mobility to be desirable because, when grounded upon meritocratic principles, it ensures that talent is effectively tapped. In addition, in offering the possibility of social betterment, it performs a stabilising function by acting as a safety-valve for the underprivileged. This is closely allied to functionalism, where goal attainment and system maintenance are the twin rationales for social action. Furthermore, it is claimed that high rates of social mobility evidence the attainment of an egalitarian society. However, Lipset and Bendix argue that *too much* social mobility may also be *dys*functonal. They view social stratification systems as multi-dimensional, so that, for example, an improvement in occupational status which is unaccompanied by a concomitant increase in social power produces overall status inconsistency. The resultant dissatisfaction may be translated into social and political instability.[1]

A point that frequently tends to be overlooked by those who believe that the goal of real equality of opportunity is an attainable one, relates to the effects of their early socialisation experience in lowering the aspirations of working-class children to become upwardly mobile. Even in a society of genuinely equal opportunities one would in any case expect the aspirations of any randomly-selected group of young men or women to show wide differences. If those in such a group were similar in level of *education*, however, it might be supposed that the proportions of those of working-class and middle-class origin aspiring to enter particular fields would be roughly the same. In practice, of course, adolescent career aspirations are so much the product of primary socialisation that this kind of rough equality is never found. Instead, in our own society, those who apply for university entrance, or enter competitions for junior administrative posts in the civil service, or whatever it may be, are *not* a random sample of young people with the requisite educational background; on the contrary, they form a sample in which the over-representation of men by comparison with women, and of those of middle-class as against working-class origin, is both very marked and very persistent. As long, therefore, as the early socialisation of girls differs so much from that of boys, and that of the children of manual workers differs as it does from that of the children of white-collar workers, the utilisation of our society's latent human talent will (even should wealth and income be much less unequally distributed) inevitably fall very far short of what might theoretically be possible.

The question as to what constitutes an egalitarian society, and as to the desirability or otherwise of social stability (given the status quo), lie at the heart of criticisms levelled at the conventional approaches to social mobility in a capitalist society. A belief in the inevitability of elite formation is widespread among the lay public as well as some social theorists— such as Pareto (see chapter 3). Such a perspective dovetails neatly with the concept of 'equality of opportunity', which, though favoured by American sociologists, is not what their (at least more radical) European counterparts mean by egalitarianism. Equality of opportunity may be rather unkindly described as what Margaret Thatcher defined equality to be some years ago: the freedom to be unequal. As Westergaard and Resler note, egalitarianism proper implies equality in the distribution of social and economic resources, which in turn implies the disappearance of social hierarchy itself.[2] The existence of social mobility precludes egalitarianism, strictly speaking. Westergaard and Resler suggests that American domination of social mobility research after 1945 accounts for the false characterisation of societies with low mobility rates as class-ridden, whilst those with high mobility rates are classless. The terms 'class' and 'classless' society relate, they argue, to the mode of production in operation, not upon the rates of mobility between classes. Furthermore, high rates of social mobility can and do accompany inequality of opportunity: chances of upward mobility for the working class may rise whilst the opportunities open to the middle class still remain superior.[3]

For those who, like Westergaard and Resler, take a Marxist perspective, the study of social mobility is useful in illuminating the operation of the social stratification system in capitalist societies, but it is essentially subordinate to the real stuff of class analysis. Once the existing social order is defined as morally undesirable, the maintenance of social stability loses all significance: it is precisely social change which is desired. Social mobility itself is undesirable insofar as it places the responsibility for success or failure upon the individual rather than on the social structure. If people *believe* equality of opportunity to exist (regardless of the facts), they can only blame themselves if they do not succeed. A blinkered chase for the elusive carrot prevents the donkey from recognising that it is surrounded by others in similar difficulties: class solidarity (the recognition of common interests) is weakened. The theme of class structuration in advanced industrial societies is currently receiving much attention; it will be taken up again in chapter 16.

HOW DOES MOBILITY AFFECT INDIVIDUALS AND FAMILIES?

The answer to such a question will relate partly to the particular route by which the individual's upward movement has taken place. The routes most usually identified are four in number. There is, first of all, securing a better than average *education*. Though this may not guarantee the opportunity of high status employment, it is increasingly becoming an essential prerequisite for those who aspire to achieve more highly regarded jobs than their fathers held. Secondly, though relatively less important than it used to be, it still sometimes happens that people with only perhaps the legal minimum of formal education are nevertheless able subsequently to *work their way* to high occupational status. Thirdly, *marrying* into a higher social setting has always been an accepted upward mobility route, and there is no obvious reason to suppose that its importance will decline. Fourthly, *financial windfalls* of many kinds if large enough, naturally, provide the economic basis for upward movement.

Leaving aside the problem of the route by which upward movement takes place, the benefits to the individual are supposed to relate to the greater scope he has for the exercise of his talents, his greater satisfaction in work, the superior life style made possible for his wife and family, and similar advantages. No one but the person immediately affected can judge how far these favourable results are outweighed by the sense of social isolation often said to be experienced by the upwardly mobile, who may feel they belong neither to the stratum from which they have moved nor to that in which they now find themselves. British novelists of the 1950s who were loosely classified as the 'angry young men' told, often in an autobiographical way, of their disillusionment on reaching the social settings to which they had aspired.[4] Musgrove, in what was intended to be a non-fictional study of social mobility, painted a horrifying picture of the types of personality that, in his view, the English educational system of the postwar era tended to select and accentuate.[5] The English grammar school forced aspiring working-class children to sacrifice their loyalties to home and neighbourhood for loyalty to the school, and only when they were prepared to do so was their advancement made possible. At every stage of ladder-climbing the characteristics associated with this 'affectionless personality', as he called it, were reinforced. When such people finally entered the various forms of local government service and other types of high status employment, they often had to move from place to place in order to secure career advancement, and so become a 'migratory elite' of lowly social origin who established no roots in the areas where they worked and lived, and whose peripatetic situation deprived them of possible support from kinsfolk. Their primary socialisation had rendered them incapable of forming satisfactory personal relationships either at work or elsewhere, so that they became more and more socially isolated and dependent solely on the very limited support they could be given from within the nuclear families they had themselves established.

Similar doubts exist regarding the balance of advantages and drawbacks so far as the families of origin of such upwardly mobile people are concerned. Jackson and Marsden and many others have illustrated the sense of bewilderment and of wanting to help, but not knowing how to do so, felt by English working-class parents whose children were getting the benefit of a grammar school or higher education quite outside their own experience.[6] Once embarked on careers, geographical as well as social isolation from the family of origin is commonly experienced, and the parents may well feel that over a large span of their children's lives they are deprived of any meaningful participation at all. This must often counterbalance any feelings of satisfaction on the grounds that their children have been more successful than they themselves have been.

Altogether, therefore, it can be seen that we do not have, and are not likely to get, the information on which to judge how far, on balance, any given degree or amount of upward or downward social mobility increases or decreases the sum total of human happiness. It has, of course, sometimes been suggested that there is less personal frustration in a social situation where one is *tied* by external factors to a particular life and work style, and can therefore blame 'the system' rather than one's own inadequacies for any failure to move out of it. And since even in the most favourable circumstances only a small minority of talented people can in practice (for all the reasons we have discussed) hope to secure better material and other advantages than their peers, the feelings of the majority, who must of necessity stay where they are, might seem more worthy both of study and of consideration.

METHODOLOGICAL DIFFICULTIES

Methodological difficulties are inevitably encountered in investigating social mobility. Before discussing some of these it should be noted that the vast majority of such studies exclude women from sample and/or analysis. Sometimes presented as a mere technical problem, the decision to exclude women is in reality a theoretical issue (see chapter 15 for a discussion of this). Meanwhile, the data presented here are to be interpreted as applying to male social mobility unless specifically stated to be otherwise. It is defensible to conclude that the status of the generalisations drawn from this research is thus merely tentative and certainly incomplete. All social mobility studies attract technical criticism, both general and specific. Restricting attention to the former, some difficulties faced in all such studies now follow.

Firstly, information is always out of date. Tracing social mobility experience accurately requires longitudinal study covering the whole of an individual's life-span. Sociologists cannot wait seventy years or more for their findings; even if they could, the data would only be of limited validity. In practice, samples are taken at one point in time and retrospective data are then collected. Retrospective data are inevitably unreliable: verification is difficult; rationalisation and bad memory blur the edges. When studying intergenerational mobility, the sample of fathers (whose occupations are the base-line from which sons' mobility is measured) is dependent upon the sample of sons. Whilst securing a representative occupational distribution of sons is possible, this cannot be guaranteed for the fathers. The result may be a false picture of temporal change in social structure and mobility rates.[7]

Secondly, the problem of what constitutes 'social position' must be faced. Occupation (and position within an occupation) has been taken as the main or sole criterion.[8] This is a pragmatic decision: such information is usually readily accessible and (at least superficially) objective; occupation does accord reasonably well with other indices of social position such as income, lifestyle, prestige and educational level. No one pretends that occupation and position within it, is an ideal index for the purpose; among the more obvious drawbacks, three may be mentioned. There is the point that new occupations and positions came into being and old ones disappear; that the relative rewards of different occupations and positions often change over a period of time; and that when comparing different societies, the same position in the same occupation may have varying significance in the two cases.

Thirdly, once occupation has been chosen, justifiably or not, as the determinant of social position, the next problem is to group all the possible occupations (and positions within them) of a national population, into a manageable number of categories or classes. Whoever does this grouping, and on whatever basis it is done, there are bound to be grounds for criticism. If, for example, an attempt is made to *validate* the allocation of occupations and positions to categories, by asking a sample of citizens to say which of those in a given list they believe are popularly regarded as of roughly equivalent status, such a validation exercise can easily be faulted. Perhaps the sample of citizens, or of the occupations on which they are asked to express an opinion, is too small or too unrepresentative. Or perhaps there is no such thing as a popular view of the relative status of a whole range of occupations in any case; any attempt at such validation is consequently futile. Who is to say, therefore, whether movement across the boundary line between any two necessarily somewhat arbitrary groups of occupations is more significant, as an index of social mobility, than movement *within* one of the groups? If society consists of a hierarchy of infinite gradations, any grouping at all is bound to be arbitrary.

Finally, recent years have seen feverish attempts to develop sophisticated methods for isolating 'real' (called 'pure' or 'exchange') mobility. This distinction arises from the fact that changes in occupational structure are known to affect social mobility rates (as we shall see below). Social mobility resulting from these has been termed 'forced' (or 'structural') mobility. Yet if the ultimate goal of studying social mobility is to learn more about class structuration on the one hand, and the extent of equality of opportunity on the other, it is only pure mobility which 'really' counts. Only this kind of mobility is held to reflect the degree of 'openness' of a society and the potential for class awareness. Noble, however, has concluded that technically, it is quite impossible to separate the two kinds of mobility because they are mutually influential in the first place; more important, he points to the irrelevance of such a separation at the level of individual experience. Can one know whether the mobility one has experienced was 'forced' or 'pure'? And would this affect one's perspective on life if one did?[9]

INTRAGENERATIONAL MOBILITY

Harris and Clausen's longitudinal study recorded that 94 per cent of the men in professional/managerial occupations in Great Britain in 1953 still belonged to the same category ten years later.[10] The majority of the worklife mobility during the decade had been experienced by routine non-manual and skilled manual respondents: of those men initially in the former category, the likelihood of subsequent upward or downward mobility did not differ; of those in the latter group, subsequent downward mobility was slightly more likely.

This study included women in its sample, calculating mobility rates in the same way as for the men— on the basis of the women's *own* occupations. They experienced less mobility overall than did the men: most mobility occurred for those initially in skilled manual occupations, and furthermore, mainly in a downward direction. Consequently, women experienced less upward mobility than did the men. Interestingly, Harris and Clausen found that mobility for both sexes typically involved not simply a job change, but also a change of employer. This accords neatly with the findings of a more recent study of single graduate women's career patterns: not only did the respondents fall behind their male peers over the years, but they were also more likely to have been made redundant or to have changed jobs for other than promotional reasons. In addition, these women were more inclined to wait for an internal promotion, whereas their male peers (who had experienced more promotion anyway) were more likely to apply for better jobs with a new employer.[11]

The 1972 Nuffield study found that half of the men from the service class (higher non-manual, professional and managerial occupations) who emerged eventually as intergenerationally stable had in fact experienced downward mobility in the interim. In other words, coming from a service-class home they had entered the labour force at a lower level and had taken an average of ten years to work their way back up to a service-class occupation. For men from working-class homes, three-quarters could be classified as having had initially working-class jobs, but by the time of the study in 1972 only half of these men had not moved upwards. Of those who finally achieved service-class status, only a minority (25 per cent) had done so by entering higher education leading directly to a high-status job. In other words, most had worked their way up.

Goldthorpe and Llewellyn[12] have concluded that, firstly, once service-class positions are secured, they guarantee staying at that level for the remainder of an individual's worklife. This is undoubtedly related to the conditions of service in many salaried professional posts: security of tenure is reasonably automatic following a probation period, for example, in the Civil Service and university teaching. Secondly, though, mobility around the intermediate occupational groups (lower-level non-manual to skilled manual) is not only more frequent than elsewhere but also is not clearly patterned. This suggests that many jobs in this range are in fact 'stepping stones' upwards and downwards, but movement among them is not perceived as particularly significant *by the movers themselves*. If more long-range mobility is subsequently experienced, the intermediate stages may be viewed as significant in retrospect. If not, then such moves are not regarded as having involved changes in social status at all.

INTERGENERATIONAL MOBILITY

The pioneering study of social mobility in Britain was undertaken by Glass and his colleagues (including one of the authors of the present book) at the London School of Economics in 1949, and until the publication of the 1972 Oxford survey, which was intended to update and extend Glass's work, this has been the source from which the majority of writers on the subject drew their information.[13] A national sample of some 10,000 adult men and women, selected so as to be representative of the different regions, of urban as against rural dwellers and of those living in settlements of varying sizes, was interviewed in 1949. Educational and occupational profiles both for respondents and their spouses were obtained as well as broadly similar information relating to their grandparents, parents and children. In the processing of the occupational data a sevenfold grouping was used which was intended to reflect generally-held views on the relative status of different occupations and positions within them. These Hall/Jones categories involved classifying occupations as professionally qualified and high administrative; managerial and executive; inspectional and higher supervisory; lower supervisory; routine non-manual and skilled manual; semiskilled manual; and unskilled manual. When an analysis was made showing, for the male respondents in each of the Hall/Jones categories, the proportion who had remained in the same category as their fathers, the highest percentage (47 per cent) was found amongst respondents in group V comprising routine non-manual and skilled manual work. It was obvious, however, that this figure did not represent the true propensity of sons in this occupational category not to have moved up or down the social scale, for the size of the percentage was clearly greatly influenced by the large numbers in the category. Some 41 per cent of all the adult male respondents fell by virtue of their occupation into this one category, so that by its sheer size the chances of remaining in the same category as your father were enormously enhanced. To enable a true picture to be obtained of the real propensity of sons to remain in the same status category as their fathers it was necessary to remove the influence of the arbitrary and confusing variable of the widely differing sizes of the status categories themselves. This was done by means of a simple statistical device, the Index of Association between the status categories of sons and fathers. This compared the number of cases where you might have expected, on a purely random relationship, to find sons in the same status categories as their fathers, with the *actual* number of such cases you did in fact find. Where the expected and actual numbers were identical, you had a state of complete or perfect mobility, where sons were not tied in any way except by pure chance to the status categories of their fathers. This was represented by a ratio of 1. The actual number was the numerator and the expected number was the denominator. If the actual number was greater than the expected number you had a state of less than perfect mobility, where more sons were apparently tied to the status category of their fathers than would have been expected on a pure chance basis. When the figures were recalculated on this more sophisticated and corrected basis, it was found that the Hall/Jones category V, far from being the *least* mobile of all the categories, was, in fact, the one most nearly approaching a situation of almost perfect mobility. The occupational groups with the greatest tendency for sons to stay in the same category as their fathers proved to be the high status occupation groups, that is Hall/Jones group I (Index 13.2) and II (Index 5.9). It is obvious that in these groups fathers were often able to buy an expensive education for their sons, and by this means, as well as through their contacts, were able to ensure that their sons were launched on careers of equally high status as their own.

The general picture that emerged, then, was of a society in which there was a good deal of movement up and down the social ladder, but where there were marked differences between the various social strata in the degree to which sons found themselves in jobs of similar social status to that of their fathers. Finally, it can be noted that, because the respondents to the study covered such a wide age-range, it was possible to investigate whether there had been any changes in the amount of social mobility over the four decades preceding the inquiry. Despite the educational and social reforms that had taken place in the period (though the 1944 Education Act was too late to have had any influence), no statistically significant increase in mobility rates could be detected. And long-range mobility (moving from the bottom to the top of the scale or vice-versa) was rare.

The 1972 Nuffield survey conducted by Goldthorpe and his colleagues at Oxford utilised both a newly-developed occupational prestige scale (Hope-Goldthorpe) and more sophisticated methods of analysis than were available to Glass.[14] In brief, it finds Britain to be a society with both high rates of social mobility and upper-class stability. Seventy two per cent of the 10,000 strong all-male sample, aged between twenty and sixty four and resident in England and Wales, had experienced social mobility of some kind. Upward mobility had been considerably more frequent than had downward mobility; but Glass's finding that long-range mobility is rare was substantiated. The significance of the manual/non-manual barrier appeared to have considerably diminished, since a quarter of those respondents of manual origin had crossed this boundary during their occupational careers. Further, if the son of working-class parents once succeeds in crossing over into the non-manual sector, he can equally as well achieve a professional as a clerical position. On the other hand, few men from professional backgrounds slide further down the scale than the routine non-manual category. Heath's assessment of the data leads him to suggest that in fact educationally unsuccessful men from higher class backgrounds tend consciously to choose skilled occupations rather than clerical work, if they can, for financial reasons. He points out that skilled apprenticeships are more like to go to educationally unsuccessful boys from white-collar homes than to their blue-collar background peers.[15] This conclusion may, however, be marred by the fact that many 'educationally unsuccessful' middle-class boys do not find their way into Heath's sub-sample as he defined it (attending an elementary or secondary modern school and leaving at the minimum age without qualifications). For this group, failure in the state system is often remedied by transfer to a private school, which may well subsequently result in a different occupational profile.

As Glass had found, the highest levels of status category self-recruitment occur at the extremes of the stratification hierarchy. But the striking difference between the 1949 and 1972 studies is that overall the social origins of the Class I (professional/managerial) respondents are nevertheless heterogeneous. Whilst those from Class I backgrounds had a fifty-fifty chance of retaining their membership in adult life, it is still the case that three-quarters of current Class I members originated from lower-level homes. Quite simply, the size of Class I has increased; and this expansion has been paralleled by a contraction of opportunities in the semi- and unskilled category, Class VII. This produces a mirror image in the composition of current Class VII membership: it is homogeneous—second-generation or longer-standing members comprise three-quarters of the total. Goldthorpe, Payne and Llewellyn conclude the most significant change in relative mobility chances to have been 'the tendency . . . for the sons of non-manual workers to have "avoided" manual employment to a progressively greater extent than have those men who originated within this contracting class.'[16]

As far as the relative chances of men from different social origins experiencing mobility are concerned, then, it is the stability revealed by the comparison of the 1949 and 1972 findings which is noteworthy. However, in looking at absolute rates of mobility, a case can be made for a trend towards more 'openness' in British society. The reason for this is plain: there is more room at the top. Opportunities in the non-manual sector as a whole have increased dramatically; this is why upward mobility exceeds downward mobility. Whatever the debate about Britain's past, society today can no longer be described as 'closed', in that higher status occupations are markedly accessible to those of lower social origins. At the same time, middle- and upper-class parents still exploit their advantages so that there is a higher probability that their children will themselves secure a position of similar or higher status as adults. With increasing opportunities at the upper end of the stratification hierarchy, however, 'barriers' (strategies of exclusion practised by the members of high-status groups) to access for those from more lowly origins become in part superfluous and inoperable, because elite groups cannot reproduce themselves in sufficent numbers to fill the expanding number of positions.[17]

To enlarge on this last point, it should be stressed that fertility and rates of social mobility are mutually influential. Banks noted that fertility began to decline (the beginning of voluntary family limitation) among upper-middle-class British families during the 1873 economic depression—not because they feared poverty, but because they realised fewer children would permit them to maintain their affluence and pass on their advantage to their children.[18] (By this time, infant and child mortality rates had begun to fall too, so that it was no longer necessary to produce many children to ensure that at least some would reach adulthood). Voluntary family limitation spread, in the course of time, to all social classes, and this brought about a secular decline in fertility which, with periodic interruptions, has continued to the present day. Within this overall decline, moreover, a social class gradient has continued to be apparent. This gradient has not, however, taken the form of a steady increase in family size proceeding from the top to the bottom of the social scale; for though at the two extremes family size differs in the expected way, the *smallest* families are always found where the wives have husbands in routine white-collar occupations (the 'unproductive clerks').[19] The most recent available figures for England and Wales are based on the 1971 Census, and show that, of women married once only before age forty-five, and who had completed ten to fourteen years of marriage by that date, the average size of family was 2.23 legitimate children for those with husbands in Class I compared with 2.56 in the case of Class V; but that the lowest fertility, 1.99, was predictably in the routine non-manual category, Class IIIN.[20] So in social mobility terms, in the current context of an expanding non-manual sector, it is inevitable that these white-collar vacancies will be filled to a significant degree by those whose childhood was spent in working-class homes, thus making up for the fertility shortfall in families with non-manual fathers.

There do appear to be, in addition, certain family-of-origin factors influencing *which* individuals from a given social level actually move. For example, upwardly mobile young people from the working class tend to come from smaller families than are typical for this level. This is undoubtedly related to the superior level of material affluence that can be maintained in a small family, and so may also be connected with the educational advantages enjoyed by children who can display more advanced linguistic and cognitive development when they go to school. It is known that first-born and only children, and those with few siblings, progress more rapidly in these areas because they interact more with adults and less with their peers.

There have, however, also been other family-of-origin characteristics that have sometimes been credited with an important bearing on which individuals from a given social group actually become upwardly mobile (though in the nature of things supporting statistical evidence can rarely be produced). Musgrove, writing about the English situation, has stressed the value of having a mother from a middle-class background who has married beneath her, and who is determined that her children shall move back into the kind of social setting which she herself enjoyed before marriage; and many studies have drawn attention to the importance of the mother's role in the educational decisions that have to be made. Swift has emphasised the importance of a lower-middle-class father whose own occupational progress has been blocked, as he sees it, by lack of paper qualifications, and who therefore urges his son to obtain these necessary certificates in order to escape the frustrations he himself has experienced. It is at least clear from this and other evidence that there is more than one type of home climate conducive to the child's educational progress. The traditional upper-middle-class family setting where education 'is valued for its liberating qualities for the individual' and 'in which the child is stimulated in a generally tolerant fashion to develop his capabilities in many directions' can no longer be thought of as the only kind of background to academic success.[21]

One of the perennial subjects of debate in the study of social mobility is the comparison in this respect of British society with other countries, especially the United States. It is commonly held to be the case that the United States is a much more open society than are other industrialised countries: that social position reflects achievement more thoroughly than elsewhere, and that access to elite groups is equally open to all. On the basis of the available research, however, rates of social mobility in America are not higher than they are in Britain, and there have been no large-scale changes in social mobility patterns over time.[22]

Turner some years ago put forward the view that the educational systems of England and the United States represented contrasting ideologies which he called respectively those of sponsored and contest mobility.[23] He hypothesised that both the designers of and the participants in the English educational system thought of it as a process of elimination at a series of fixed stages. At each such stage those in authority selected the young people they judged to have the qualities considered necessary to benefit from the scarcer types of education and ultimately to fill elite positions. Those favoured in this way were chosen as early as possible, while others, found unsuitable by the judges, dropped out of the race for good and accepted the justice of such a decision. These, as Turner saw it, were the characteristics of sponsored mobility. By contrast, the American system was intended, and perceived, to keep everyone in the race as long as possible, and re-entry after having previously dropped out was not only quite in order but also meritorious. Sponsors were neither needed nor available; those who reached the top did so by their own efforts, and were entitled to use any reasonable method to get there. This was contest mobility, and could be likened to the assault course type of contest familiar as part of the selection process in the armed services, where one survived as best one could in overcoming a series of obstacles in ways of one's own choosing. Sponsored mobility, on the other hand, could be likened to a beauty contest where a once-for-all decision was made by a group of judges.

Changes that have taken place in England's arrangements since Turner wrote, such as the reorganisation of secondary education on comprehensive lines and the creation of the Open University, have blurred the contrast that Turner was seeking to make; and critics have not been slow to point out that for Negro and other ethnic minority children in the United States a sponsored rather than a contest model was a better assessment of the true position. Moreover Kerckhoff, in a comparative reanalysis of data from both countries, has concluded that as far as the influence that the kind of educational system of a country has upon its social stratification system is concerned, Britain and the United States use quite different mechanisms to bring about roughly the same outcomes. The overall amounts of intergenerational mobility are similar, as are the relative contributions respectively of social origin and ability to educational attainment.[24]

There is one striking feature of US mobility patterns not so far mentioned, namely the extent to which black Americans lag behind whites in the contest to enter high status occupations, even given comparable levels of education. As far as access to elite groups is concerned, Lieberson and Carter report, after studying *Who's Who* entries between 1924 and 1974, that black American rates of representation remain low, although they have been on the rise since the Second World War. In the earlier decades covered by the study, it was only possible for black Americans to 'make it' via success in formerly racially-segregated spheres of activity: education and religion. These routes retain their importance today, but black American representation in sports and show business have gained in significance. These latter would nevertheless not be so important proportionately, were black Americans not so under-represented in other spheres (such as law and politics, the economic elite, etc.).[25] The authors conclude that the greater success of white ethnic immigrant groups in America (e.g. Slavs, Italians) in securing access to elite groups results from their use of their 'high culture' as a pathway to distinction, since it was considered a part of the Western tradition. Little esteem was accorded to the distinctive aspects of black American culture.

Finally, to return to the British scene, the 1972 findings have sparked off a renewed debate over the implications of high rates of upward social mobility and the consequent heterogeneity of the middle class in contrast with the homogeneity of the working class. Discussion centres around two issues: the likelihood of intensified class conflict or otherwise and the notion of 'proletarianisation' (the suggestion that many non-manual occupations have become more akin to manual ones). These topics will be taken up in chapter 16. Meanwhile, we can turn to a consideration of the ways in which people try to reach the top, and the role of education in this respect.

ROUTES TO UPWARD MOBILITY

Goldthorpe and his colleagues identified three main routes of access to Class I occupations: grammar school attendance; promotion from the shop-floor; and inheritance of privilege—in descending order of *numerical* frequency. This does not contradict the fact, though, that, *relatively* speaking, children from privileged backgrounds still have enormous advantages in the competition for both Class I and *elite* positions. Heath has calculated that the chances of getting into *Who's Who* in Britain vary as follows: for the working-class boy, 1 in 1,500; for the middle-class boy, 1 in 500; for the boy whose father is in a professional/managerial occupation, 1 in 200; and for the son of a member of an elite group, 1 in 5.[26]

But the degree of openness of different elites varies. Self-employed professionals are the most exclusive social recruiters; they are easily the best educated of all Class I members, and are much more likely to have attended elite private schools; they are most likely to have occupied Class I jobs from the point of labour-force entry. Since the beginning of the nineteenth century there does seem to have been a general, though slow and uneven, movement towards greater openness in access to elite groups, but the pace of reform varies considerably between elites. The Civil Service and the Armed Forces have opened up considerably; but while in industry salaried professional management is ascendant, the inheritance of wealth is still very significant at the top levels. The City, however, is even today a bastion of privilege.[27]

While the 1972 Nuffield findings do demonstrate that cycles of privilege continue to exist, they do not support the notion that transmitted social deprivation exists on a large scale in modern Britain. A group representing about 5 per cent of the population can be shown to exist who suffer from multiple social disadvantage, but of their representatives in the Nuffield sample, fewer than half failed to achieve some measure of upward mobility. What is the case, however, is that those from working-class backgrounds, and especially from semi- and unskilled homes, seem to be born to fail *educationally*.[28] This is important, since educational attainment is known to influence occupational achievement, though to what extent is uncertain.

Halsey, Heath and Ridge,[29] in a separate investigation using the Nuffield data, have been able to show that educational qualifications increase the chances of upward social mobility, whereas the lack of these is connected with the experience of downward mobility. Meritocratic principles *do* play a role in shifts in the composition of social class groupings. But it is quite clear that inequality of opportunity by social class has eased little since 1900. A case can be made for an approximation to meritocracy up until the minimum school-leaving age (if the class bias in IQ performance is discounted), but thereafter working class disadvantage reasserts itself with a vengeance.

The widespread belief that expansion of, and equality in, educational opportunity can remodel the unacceptable face of social stratification by replacing ascription with achievement does not fit the facts and is anyway unrealistic. To use the title of a widely-read article by Bernstein, 'Education cannot compensate for Society'. Changing the rules of the game does not affect its ultimate rationale: somebody wins and somebody loses. And, to conclude with a metaphor, the Briton who plays Scrabble in English with a German will, all other things being equal, almost always win: 'cultural capital' tells.[30] Playing the game by the rules is no substitute for knowing your way around.

Sexual stratification and social stratification 15

That this chapter exists at all reflects two important facts: sexual divisions are socially significant, and relations between the sexes are stratified. In principle, all sociological analysis should integrate sexual divisions on an equal basis; in practice, little does this, all too frequently because it is pervaded with the same ideology which informs everyday relationships between the sexes. Bluntly, sociological analysis is all too often sexist. *Because* relationships between the sexes in advanced industrial societies (and in others) are characterised not only by complementarity but also by hierarchical opposition, the social sex category in sociology is 'ignored by some and denied by others'.[1] Nowhere is this more in evidence than in the study of social stratification. There can be no doubt that sexual stratification exists: there are systematic inequalities of access, in favour of men, to the critical dimensions of rewards, prestige and power. Yet, although the fact of sexual inequality as a form of social disadvantage has been more or less acknowledged, there has been a reluctance, even refusal, to incorporate this variable fully into theoretical and empirical analyses of social stratification.

This chapter addresses the following questions: How has conventional stratification theory and research justified the essential irrelevancy it accords to women? Why is this unacceptable? What attempts to resolve this problem have been put forward? What empirical evidence can be brought to bear upon women's position in the social stratification system?

SEXUAL DIVISIONS IN STRATIFICATION THEORY AND RESEARCH

The definition of the family as the unit of the stratification system and the reliance upon men's occupations as the crucial articulators of the relationship between the family and the class structure are the twin assumptions guiding theorists and investigators. This has led to at least three distinct theoretical positions. Parkin represents the view that sexual stratification is irrelevant to social stratification theory. The division of labour between the sexes may be at the root of sexual inequality, but it cannot explain class inequality. Women, furthermore, cannot be said to form a cohesive social group, i.e. they do not demonstrate 'class' solidarity.[2] The occupational structure *is* significant. For example, the more non-manual jobs there are, the larger the middle class, which may affect class relationships and inequalities.

The second perspective, held by Giddens,[3] takes account of the fact that the occupational structure is heavily sexually segregated (women and men are not generally employed in the same occupations). This is an *effect* of sexual inequality and as such may influence aspects of class structure. For example, the fact that routine non-manual work is staffed primarily by women affects the nature of the boundary between the middle and working class. The low pay and inferior conditions, yet formal white-collar status, of such occupations, turn their incumbents into an 'underclass' which acts as a 'buffer zone' preventing upward mobility for the working class. Nevertheless, women's primary role location and secondary status within the family ensure that their employment remains of subsidiary relevance to themselves, to household income and to the economy. Until women are liberated from the family, they cannot be of more than peripheral relevance to the class system.

Westergaard and Resler's Marxist analysis provides us with the third position.[4] They agree that men's socio-economic position is much more important than that of women for the purposes of class analysis. However, the significance of sexual inequality lies in its role as *accentuating* class inequalities. On the one hand, the differences in income levels between women employed in higher-status versus low-status occupations are *wider* than those for men; on the other, working-class women are employed under the most exploitative conditions. Their wages are vital to the family budget, but wives' earnings still cannot eliminate the gap between middle-class and working-class average household incomes.

The outcome of all three perspectives is similar: social stratification research has typically relegated women to a position of secondary interest, or simply excluded them altogether. This latter is indeed the most serious and fundamental flaw in the design of the 1972 Nuffield social mobility survey (see chapter 14). Goldthorpe, the senior investigator, has defended the decision to exclude women from the sample by maintaining that it is men, through their occupations and incomes, who determine to which class their families belong. He points out that husbands almost always possess higher-status and better-paying jobs than do their wives; and a family adopts the highest status available to it. In any case, since the time-period referred to in this study, like all social mobility projects, works backwards from the date of investigation—in this case, before 1972—it can safely be assumed that married women in employment were never in the majority in comparison with those who were housewives alone.[5]

Studies of class identity and political behaviour take a similar stance. One recent study of class consciousness, claiming general significance for its conclusions, included a sample of clerical workers for investigation. The influx of women in to this field and the concomitant deterioration in pay and conditions has engendered one of the hottest debates in class analysis today (see chapter 16 on 'proletarianisation'), but this study does not address this issue at all.
The sample was exclusively male, although the author notes that 90 per cent of the workers in the departments from which the respondents were drawn were female.[6] Similarly, conventional studies of political participation have claimed that women are less interested in politics than are men, and that on this basis women's political views and voting patterns are of subsidiary interest.[7]

There is one area of social stratification research which has not only integrated sexual divisions into its rationale but also *focuses* on women: the study of marital mobility—marrying 'up' and 'down'. Conventionally, this is what comprises social mobility for women, which accords with the perspectives revealed above. But, Heath notes, since a woman's social class before marriage has traditionally been measured by her father's occupation, marital mobility studies are actually investigating the relationship between a man's social class and that of his father-in-law.[8]

In sum, the stratification literature makes the following assumptions: The family is the unit of the stratification system, and its social position can only be determined by the male head of the household. Women live in families, which means that their class position is identical to their husband's or father's. Finally , women determine their own social position only when they are not attached to a man.[9] But is all this valid or useful?

DIFFICULTIES RAISED BY CONVENTIONAL APPROACHES

To take the nuclear family as the unit of social stratification may be justifiable for certain purposes, but it provides us with an immediate problem: not everybody lives in a family. Currently, in both the United States and Britain, about one-third of households do not fit the nuclear family model. Twenty per cent alone consists of single-persons. It has had to be accepted in conventional research that when women live alone, or in households with no male head, their own occupations must be and are used to determine their own and the household's class position. It is illogical to permit women to determine their own and their family's class position in *some* circumstances but not in others. We know that in households where both spouses are employed the occupations of *both* influence at least the social status awarded by others to the household as a unit (although the husband's occupation *is* given more weight).[10] Women's educational attainment and occupational status, before and after marriage, have a significant influence both on their husband's occupational and their children's educational attainments, which cannot but be relevant for social mobility.[11]

To maintain that only men's occupations are relevant for the family's class position is, then, untenable. Equally as problematic is the assertion that all family members share the same social position.

To begin with, married women's employment is not unusual at all: approximately 45 per cent of the labour force in Britain and the USA is female. For women from the lower social classes, employment has never been unusual. Women's occupational distribution *is*, however, different from men's: they are crowded into routine non-manual occupations and are seriously under-represented in the higher professional/managerial groups and amongst skilled manual workers. This arises from dissimilar job opportunities; but its unavoidable consequence is that for households where both spouses are employed, there is a low overall correlation between husband's and wife's social class position.[12] (The peculiar occupational distribution of women is also, incidentally, responsible for the sharper income gradient amongst employed women, which led Westergaard and Resler to assert that sexual stratification merely accentuates class inequalities.)

It is the rigid adherence to the occupational system *alone* as the framework for class analysis which is the source of the difficulties. It *is* the case that women's work, both within and outside the home, does not fit this framework well; but it is *not* true that the occupational structure is immune to the influence of purely social variables. For example, technological change affects occupational structure, as where the development of computers has created new occupations (computer programmers) and is eliminating old ones (filing clerks). But the costs of investing in new technology may not be worthwhile if labour continues to be cheaply available. Women are traditionally a source of cheap labour; and they are so because of their disadvantaged position in the division of labour within the family.[13]

All these problems have led some sociologists, and especially feminist sociologists, to demand a reconceptualisation of stratification theory and a rejuvenation of research initiatives.

TOWARDS A REDEFINITION OF THE ISSUES

Those who are involved in the theoretical reformulation of the relationship between sexual stratification and social stratification are unanimous in the verdict that it is the division of labour between the sexes, and especially that within the family, which is the key to the problem. Beyond this, opinions diverge. One view, stemming from the cross-cultural data collected by social anthropologists, sees the division of labour by sex as a necessary but not sufficent cause of sexual stratification.[14] Where tasks are allocated differentially by sex, the basis exists for economic inequality between men and women insofar as some tasks may be more highly regarded and rewarded than are others. This then leads to power inequalities. But if the valued tasks are shared out equally, and if control over the products of one's labour is equally distributed, this will not happen.

Others argue that sex membership itself is not only used as a rationale for the allocation of tasks and for inequality between men and women, but is an independent contributor to social status. Sexual stratification cross-cuts class stratification: they are independent systems of social ranking, and an integrative solution would be to regard women as 'castes' within classes.[15] This perspective contains elements of the two major, and rival, approaches to the topic to have surfaced in the past decade.

The 'socialist feminist' approach incorporates the following points.[16] Firstly, whilst women may not, as Parkin says, act as a cohesive social group, this is equally true of male workers. It is not surprising that women do not recognise that most of them, in terms of their conditions of life, are members of the working class: their social position is indeed more ambiguous than that of men, who in any event are still subject to regarding women as subordinate to themselves. It is difficult to feel a sense of common interest with those who regard one as inferior. Secondly, although a high proportion of women are to be found in the non-manual sector, they are mostly at the level of clerical and sales work, so that income and work conditions are such as to cast serious doubt on whether such occupations can meaningfully be labelled middle class. Many problems would be resolved if it were accepted that most women's occupations are really working class in character. Thirdly, social classes are not homogeneous masses—there *are* sub-groups in special situations, and women are such a sub-group. They have a unique place in the stratification system, arising from their vulnerability both within the home and on the labour market.

This perspective, then, suggests that women constitute a 'class within a class'. The 'radical feminist' view goes further: it suggests that women constitute a 'class in its own right'. To call women 'working class' or 'middle class' at all is inaccurate; these concepts, among others, belong to conventional social stratification theory, which accords women no legitimate, independent social position of their own. Women's real class interests lie in solidarity with other women; if they do not realise this, then it can be said that they are suffering from 'false consciousness' in just the same way as the steelworker who votes Conservative is held to be, in some circles. In essence, women do not fit into the conventional frameworks of class analysis, and therefore the frameworks are inappropriate. It is patriarchy which is relevant for the analysis of sexual stratification—and patriarchy precedes capitalism, historically speaking. Convention is turned on its head: sexual inequality is merely accentuated by class inequality.[17]

WOMEN AND SOCIAL STRATIFICATION: WHAT DO WE KNOW?

That women suffer serious social disadvantage in both educational and occupational opportunity is well documented.[18] Three aspects of this disadvantage are discussed here: social mobility, occupational attainment and status, and the feminisation of occupations.

There is a scarcity of data on women's social mobility: what exists is tentative, given the inadequacies of research design (e.g. social origins judged on the basis of father's occupation alone). First, let us dispose of marital mobility. American and British data provide no support for the notion that women are disproportionately inclined to marry up. There is a good deal of marrying up *and* down for both sexes, with the net result that no identifiable trend in either direction is observable. It may be that a few women of high social class background remain single rather than accept marrying down;

and conversely, men from working-class homes are at a slight disadvantage on the marriage market.[19] The question has, however, been posed as to whether marriage *per se* is an exercise in potential or actual downward mobility for women: married women's status is low, especially if they devote themselves exclusively to the socially devalued role of housewife.[20]

Patterns of occupational mobility in Britain differ considerably between the sexes. Because of the crowding of women into routine non-manual and semi-unskilled occupations, it is inevitable that although women (like men) currently experience more upward than downward mobility, the difference between the two rates is very small. In that women are under-represented in high-status occupations, it is particularly noticeable that women from high-level social origins are downwardly mobile in large numbers. Sons of high-status fathers are prone to follow in their footsteps—but this is not so for daughters.[21] Clearly, social class background is not related to occupational attainment in the same way for women as it is for men. A recent British study observed that cultural capital had played a role in the careers of male graduates from high social class backgrounds; although the social origins of their female peers were on average higher, they did not benefit from this and their occupational attainments were lesser.[22] The lower-level professional occupations of schoolteaching, social work, librarianship and graduate nursing do offer a channel of upward mobility for single educated women in particular. But this channel could not be used by many more women, for supply already exceeds demand.

Women are so likely to be found in routine non-manual occupations that they are prone to end up there regardless of social origin. Consequently, women's differential access to very high-status and very low-status jobs *by contrast* reveals the strong influence of social origin upon occupational attainment.[23] (Yet another reason why class inequalities have appeared sharper among employed women than men in traditional analyses.) Although it is true that women find access to white-collar work easier than do men, it is important to remember that the vast majority of the jobs they are offered are not very desirable in terms of the rewards and prestige attached to them. Nevertheless, women will avoid work in the manual sector where possible, because the occupations here to which they have access are even worse by the same criteria. The end result is that women from white-collar backgrounds are almost always able to find jobs in that sector themselves, whilst women from working-class homes will fill jobs in *both* sectors.

North American research uniformly finds education to be especially significant for women's chances of upward social mobility, because other channels are relatively closed to them.[24] This is why, for example, women are well advised to select occupations where the rules for entry and promotion are clearly specified, such as the Civil Service. They cannot expect to enjoy effective equality of opportunity even here, but they can minimise their disadvantage.[25]

During the 1960s, educational expansion followed by economic recession was experienced in both Europe and North America. A Canadian study, tracing the occupational fortunes of university graduates through the decade, found that both sexes benefited from the initial higher demand for graduates and suffered from its subsequent sharp fall-off. However, regardless of the year of graduation, women experienced less upward mobility than did men. When demand is high, women make some gains—though not so many as do men; when demand slackens, men suffer relatively more—though their chances remain better than those of women. Similarly, even when employers are eager to absorb all the highly-qualified labour they can obtain, women are still obliged to provide more proof of their abilities than are men (by, for example, having postgraduate qualifications). The authors of this study concluded that 'fewer tracks and a harder race' characterise female mobility and occupational attainment patterns.[26]

With reference to prestige, the occupational structure comprises a pair of 'sex-specific, parallel hierarchies' modified by the fact that the very prestigious male-dominated occupations have no female-dominated counterparts. The sex composition of an occupation as such does not, apparently, affect its prestige rating. But this approximation to equality in access to occupational prestige has little real meaning, since women and men rarely actually meet as equals at work. When the sexes are directly in contact, the doctor-nurse model is the preferred norm.[27] The case of the male nurse is an instructive example of what happens when this norm is upset: people find it difficult to accept the situation and do not know how to respond. They try to reassert 'normality' by suggesting that the nurse 'is really a doctor' or even by insinuating that he is 'gay'. Typically, to re-establish convention and respect, male nurses strive to obtain supervisory and prestigious nursing posts.[28] (It is noticeable that men are disproportionately represented in the new nursing degree courses in Britain.) Fundamentally, the problem arises from the inevitable coupling of prestige with power; for women to posses more power than men is highly contranormative, which accounts for the difficulties women have in securing deference from subordinates in a mixed-sex work environment. When a woman's superior power must be acknowledged, it tends to be explained away by claims that the woman concerned is 'exceptional' or 'like a man'.

The distribution for women and men among occupational status levels is always divergent, but the contrasts vary over time. Regardless of occupational aspirations, when women first enter the labour-force, they are on average likely to obtain higher-prestige jobs than their male peers (although the reverse holds for those with degrees). This arises from the disproportionate absorption of women in the lower levels of the white-collar sector. But by the time they are in their mid-thirties, the superior upward mobility chances of men occasion a dramatic change in the picture: not only have men overtaken women in the occupational prestige stakes, but women have, on average, lost ground. The jobs they now occupy tend to be of lower status than their first jobs were. This is not wholly due to the interruptions occasioned by childbearing, for even women who have remained childless have gained little occupational status over the course of their working lives.[29]

That women are rarely to be found among the ranks of elites is a matter of common knowledge. Observation of the situation suggests that women are only tolerated as members of ingroups insofar as they do not try to claim key positions; they tend to be allocated to less influential areas which are typically associated with 'women's interests', such as health and welfare. On the other hand, their access to elites has been improved in absolute terms by the very introduction of equal opportunity and affirmative action legislation—they fill the government and commercial posts promoting and monitoring these initiatives. The traditional access route for women has been 'widow's succession' (for example, when a wife or daughter is appointed to a man's position after his death); a channel of increasing significance is that caused by the rise in power and status of 'experts' in a high-technology society and economy. The need for expertise overrides concern over the sex of the technocrat.[30]

The final dismantling of sex inequality of formal access to prestigious educational institutions (e.g. the Ivy League colleges, Oxbridge) and the sharp rise in the number of female law students (especially in the USA) should in future facilitate an increase in women's membership of political elites. In the USA these act as springboards for political office, and being a lawyer gives a woman 'instant credibility'. It also helps to ameliorate the problems women have in achieving integration into the informal networks of communication and patronage which is essential to successful career development.[31]

Finally, the sex composition of an occupation *does* affect economic rewards: the higher the proportion of women in an occupation, the larger the gap between the salaries of men and women in that occupation. When women's representation in an occupation increases, its market value indisputably declines.[32] This must reflect the concentration of men in the highest-paying posts, but also the assessment of women's labour as more cheaply available (which it is, given their social and economic vulnerability). The *feminisation* of an occupation (when a formerly male-dominated occupation becomes primarily staffed by women) typically arises from employer-initiated rationalisation of organisational structure and work tasks. In the United States after 1945, banking was reorganised; one of the outcomes was that the position of bank clerk no longer constituted the first step on the career ladder. Those destined for high-ranking position were taken in at a higher level, which effectively blocked the bank clerk's promotion chances permanently. Supported by the assessment of women's employment as subsidiary in nature, banking companies redefined the formerly male-dominated occupation of bank clerk into a 'glamorous'—but less prestigious and well-paid—occupation for women. The introduction of advanced technology consolidated the change: a job formerly regarded as one demanding responsibility and intelligence is now defined as routine and methodical.[33] In Britain, a crisis in the general insurance business from the mid-1950s onwards precipitated a similar process of rationalisation and concentration, resulting in the creation of a new office proletariat. Insurance companies today employ armies of semi-skilled data processers and a small 'officer corps' of managers. The latter are not recruited from the former.[34] Not surprisingly, the proportion of insurance employees who are women has risen—but needless to say, few are to be found in the executive suite.

Themes of current debate 16

Inevitably, earlier chapters have hinted at the debates which have arisen as a result of the data thrown up by empirical research into social stratification. Here, some of the more topical of these are discussed; all raise questions in some way about change or lack of change in patterns of structured social inequality in advanced industrial societies.

CONVERGENCE OR DIVERGENCE?

American sociologists in particular have in the past supported the thesis that industrialisation has deep-seated, unavoidable and universal effects upon a society and its culture.[1] It is argued that technology exerts an invariable influence upon occupational structure, which then affects social stratification systems; finally, occupation itself influences individuals' attitudes and behaviour. The striving for efficiency which characterises modern economic systems demands rationalisation of the methods of occupational allocation: those most able and best qualified for a position are chosen to fill it. Thus industrial societies are increasingly universalistic, or achievement-oriented, which produces higher rates of social mobility and equality of opportunity. In particular, industrialisation accelerates the expansion of the middle class and the consequent fractionalisation of the stratification system: the hierarchy comprises a series of finely-gradated levels with no sharp breaks, easier communication and movement between them. In a schema proposed by Goldthorpe some years ago, industrial societies can be seen as more 'open' on the *mobility* dimension, as becoming more 'middle class' on the *differentiation* dimension, and as more stable, in that advanced technology tends to produce status consistency for any one person, on the *consistency* dimension.[2] There is still little evidence for this last hypothesis; Goldthorpe himself has modified his ideas on 'openness' subsequent to his 1972 Nuffield study; and the characterisation of advanced industrial societies as 'middle class' has proved distinctly problematic on both theoretical and empirical levels.

The enthusiasm for a strong version of the convergence thesis has waned considerably. At a high level of generality, it is quite clear that industrial societies are similar: they all have a technologically complex division of labour, an industrially-oriented workforce, comparable demographic structures, nuclear family-based kinship patterns, and so on. But below the surface social, cultural and political variations are immediately observable (the difference between Canada and the United States is a salutary example). These differences influence patterns of economic structure and development themselves. Garnsey[3] argues that technology is not an independent variable; neither are market forces all-powerful. Advanced industrial societies tend towards a dominance of the services sector as employer of the labour force, towards an expansion in the proportion of higher-level occupations and towards a general upgrading and specialisation of workforce skills. But to conclude that the occupational distributions of such societies are identical, and are *determined* by technology and market forces is incorrect. The Soviet Union's economy is not 'backward' in comparison with other advanced industrial nations on the whole, but its occupational distribution is quite different: a high proportion of the workforce is still employed in agriculture, and the most highly-skilled technical occupations account for a higher percentage of workers than in the West; but services, management and administration occupy a much smaller share of the labour force. This pattern is the direct result of government policy, based on social and political ideology: the non-manual and service sectors are regarded as largely useless; rural to urban migration has been deliberately discouraged.

Blau and Duncan's[4] conclusion that industrial societies are all characterised by a trend towards expanding universalism, on the basis of data they collected on the American occupational structure, has been shown to have only limited validity for Britain at any rate. Education *has* become more important for the transmission of social status from parents to children, because educational attainment and occupational opportunity have indeed become more closely related. But at the same time social origins and educational attainment appear to be more closely correlated than they used to be, which may surprise some. So, the rules have changed, but the inequality remains: middle-class parents use education instead of nepotism to assure their children's futures.[5]

Earlier comparative studies of social mobility rates disagreed over whether industrial societies are similar in *this* respect or not.[6] A recent comparison[7] of nineteen industrial societies, taking up the ideas that 'newly-founded' and left-wing governed societies will show higher rates of social mobility, was able to produce tentative support for both (and especially the latter) hypotheses. In addition, highly traditional societies with a history of right-wing political domination all display lower rates of social mobility than would have been predicted on the basis of their occupational distribution (West Germany, Spain, Italy, Japan). Similarly, whilst the elites of all advanced industrial societies are heterogeneous in terms of their members' social origins, the likelihood of long-range upward mobility into elites differs sharply—for example, in Italy chances are small, whereas in Hungary they are quite good. But comparing Britain and the USA, as we have seen, does not show any startling differences as far as social mobility is concerned. We can only concur with the view that much more research is needed before the ultimate validity of convergence and divergence hypotheses can be safely determined.

THE CONCEPT OF CLASS

Controversy over the precise meaning and degree of usefulness of the term 'class' is a favourite pastime of the sociologist. Aside from never-ending debates over how to operationalise the concept, two kinds of issues provoke insatiable appetites into action: whether it is significant for the validity of the concept that ordinary people are *aware* of class divisions and their own place within these; and whether a Marxist-oriented analysis of social stratification is any longer useful.

Wrong[8] claims that before we can legitimately speak of a 'class' we have to be able to identify a large group of people with major economic interests in common together with a consciousness of this and of their relation to the structure as a whole. Except in the case of ethnic minorities, such groups cannot be identified in contemporary America, which is therefore to be regarded as a classless society—but which nevertheless displays both social inequality and social mobility. He is essentially objecting to the tendency of sociologists to draw arbitrary lines around particular groups of people similarly situated in some respect, and call them classes. Marwick, from the standpoint of a social historian making a comparative study of the image and reality of class in Britain, France and the USA since 1930, thinks in much the same way: he says he prefers class to mean what people in everyday life mean by it rather than what eminent sociologists tell him to mean by it.[9] His observations, however, lead him to disagree with Wrong's claim that the United States is a classless society. Contemporary American sociology is united, by and large, in its view of the social stratification system as a kind of continuously moving escalator, but within this, the most recent sociological study affirms that there are indeed three classes (upper, middle and lower) to be distinguished in the United States today.[10] The average American takes the possession of material goods to be the all-important indicator of class membership, so that in spite of the continued significance of the collar-colour distinction, a manual worker who maintains a white-collar lifestyle will be socially accepted as an equal.

The language of class is in wider usage in the United States than it used to be; but the astonishing capacity of Americans to weld almost everyone into an undifferentiated 'middle class' remains truly remarkable. A more sophisticated perception and usage of the class concept is prevented in the United States by the greater salience of occupational demarcations, sectionalism, and, in particular, race.[11] This fits in with Giddens' suggestion that class formation in general may be hindered by asserting the primacy of other social divisions; at the same time, these divisions may be used to create an 'underclass' of especially exploited persons who have little chance of securing upward mobility because they possess an ascribed attribute which disqualifies them from doing so.[12]

Americans still criticise Britain as being class-ridden. In terms of the actual extent of social inequality, the two countries do not, as we have seen, appreciably differ. But on the level of people's perceptions of the significance of class, the judgement is probably a fair one. Bottomore[13] contends that social classes *do* play an important role in all aspects of economic and political life, although the constellation of the system is no longer as it was when Marx was writing. The continued importance of class consciousness, as evidenced by militant union action, suggests to him that the claim that the class concept has no contemporary relevance is invalid. Marwick concludes (from the study referred to earlier) that in Britain 'class is alive and well', if less fixed in character. There is a well-defined upper class or elite, there has been a flowering of middle class self-consciousness,[14] and the working class retains for the most part a strong sense of self-confidence in its own identity. If Marwick is correct, it seems that in the United States the class concept has insinuated itself rather more into social consciousness than used to be the case, whereas all are agreed that British perceptions are more varied and fuzzy than they formerly were. Yet a survey of the research literature on class perceptions and social imagery leads Noble to state that class has little salience in Britons' worldviews or order of matters for concern nowadays; class distinctions carry 'no great burden of social or political commitment'.[15] Westergaard disagrees: he finds that 'the potential for social protest is at least as likely to be growing as declining', for the gap between aspirations and achievements remains wide in the context of persistent inequality of opportunity.[16]

Giddens has delivered one of the more notable theoretical contributions to the general issue, attacking the problematic of the irreconcilable disparity between Marxist and Weberian approaches.[17] Both are inadequate: Marx's dichotomous model cannot conceptualise the middle class; Weber's model theoretically permits an infinity of classes, which is unrealistic and unwieldy. Giddens's reformulation assumes that workers are *not* propertyless: their property is their labour power, which is essential to the employer.[18] This property he then renames as 'market capacity', its value varying primarily with the level of skill a worker can offer. A resulting infinity of economic relationships is transformed into a given number of social classes (whose boundaries are inherently fuzzy) by what he calls 'class structuration' processes. The overall transformation links ('mediate structuration factors') consist of the distribution of social mobility chances, which is influenced by private ownership, educational qualifications, and the value of labour power itself. These mediate factors are modified in their pure effects by a further set of variables ('proximate structuration factors') which operate at a localised, specific level. They comprise variations in the division of labour and authority relationships in the workplace on the one hand, and the emergence of status groups based on differing patterns of consumption on the other. He concludes that the manner in which all these factors combine is, at one level, similar in all advanced industrial capitalist societies: the result is a three-class system (upper, middle and working), but which allows for the influence of a nation's specific political and economic situation and for the existence of sub-groups within the major classes. There can be no doubt that Giddens has clarified some issues and presented us with useful insights; but to suggest that the issues have been thereby fully resolved would be quite misleading—this debate is rather like the yellow-brick road, it goes on for ever.

EMBOURGEOISEMENT AND PROLETARIANISATION

The embourgeoisement thesis states that the increasing affluence enjoyed as a result of the advances in technology by certain groups of workers leads them virtually to move into the middle class as far as lifestyles, aspirations and attitudes are concerned. What is being suggested is that *stratum mobility* has occurred: a whole category of workers and their families have experienced upward social mobility. The evidence for this was said to lie in three main factors: higher income levels, an increase in home-centredness, and a swing towards more conservative political views. The major empirical test of this hypothesis, a study of highly-paid Luton car assembly workers, did not support this thesis fully.[19] It is true that these affluent workers took a much more restricted view of the value of trade unionism; like their approach to their jobs in general, these workers adopted an instrumental attitude. Unions' goals should be to obtain better wages and shop-floor conditions; the job was a means of earning as much money as possible. It was also the case that the car-workers were very much home-centred: they placed value on home-ownership and improvement; they were oriented towards the acquisition of material goods. But more significantly, these workers had no aspirations for upward social mobility and had little social contact with the established middle class. In addition, although income levels for such groups of workers are higher than for the rest of the working class and for lower-level non-manual employees, they do not enjoy the fringe benefits and job security which are automatically provided for white-collar workers. The authors concluded that what had occurred was that sections of the working and middle classes were converging on a normative level, but certainly not assimilating. The affluent workers are a prototype 'new working class'.

It has been pointed out that the term 'embourgeoisement' is a misnomer anyway: propertyless 'affluent' manual workers are converging with propertyless white-collar workers (if with any group at all), whereas the term 'bourgeois' can only be applied to those who have a stake in the ownership of the means of production. Westergaard has made the caustic comment that instrumentalism is nothing new—that embourgeoisement theorists have merely 'rediscovered the cash-nexus'.[20] Others claim the 'new worker' to be nothing new either—today's 'old working class' areas were once viewed as being populated by a new species too. Affluent workers have not really changed their class position: they are still virtually or wholly propertyless and their labour power is still at the mercy of the market.[21] The affluent workers are simply making a pragmatic accommodation to the realities of life in an advanced industrial society: they are prepared to take on boring and unpleasant jobs as long as they are paid sufficient to finance a comfortable lifestyle, which they view as otherwise inaccessible to them.

The thesis of *proletarianisation* has attracted more attention since embourgeoisement has fallen into disfavour. The de-skilling of many lower-level non-manual jobs following the application of advanced technology to office procedures, and the mooted decline in autonomy for the salaried professional, have been suggested as the factors which are precipitating a recognition on the part of the non-manual workforce that they, too, are part of the proletariat. This should, it is claimed, eventually lead to mass action to overthrow the existing social system.

It is certainly the case that some groups of professional workers are much more politically radical than their class position would traditionally imply (university lecturers, for example), and it is noticeable that the social origins of European terrorists are typically distinctly middle class. It is also true that the middle class as such has become more 'militant' (though not necessarily in a left-wing direction): they see themselves as the major contributors to the welfare state, and at the same time perceive that their traditional position of economic superiority in comparison with manual workers is being eroded. In consequence, they are adopting the notion that forms of protest traditionally and successfully used by the working class via trade unionism can be appropriate for them too. A further point can legitimately be made. There is no doubt that routine non-manual work has been dramatically affected by automation and rationalisation, marked by a deterioration in pay and all aspects of work conditions. (It is often argued that automation creates more responsible jobs requiring a higher level of qualifications. This may be true, but the corollary, that thereby routine non-manual jobs are being eliminated, is certainly not universally valid.)

The tendency of professional sub-groups to espouse political radicalism is difficult to interpret; we have virtually no data to go on. But it does seem unlikely that high status occupational groups as a whole will move in this direction in the near future. The United States has the highest proportion of highly-qualified scientific and technical personnel in its workforce, but upper-middle class radicalism is not noticeably in evidence. Current perspectives on the middle class tend either to claim increasing fragmentation into sub-groups with divergent interests, or to place its members in a 'no man's land' characterised by lack of any consciousness at all. It is undeniable that rates of white-collar unionisation have increased significantly in recent years. However, it seems that the main factors involved are the expanding scale of industrial enterprises with resultant concentration of employees in large blocks, and the rising recognition of non-manual unions by both government and employers (which may have helped to allay anxieties over the potential damage to individual promotion prospects caused by joining a union).[22] There is, furthermore, little evidence that non-manual workers and their unions are interested in much more than purely sectional interests—the restoration of differentials and the maintenance of a generally privileged position.

Where individual white-collar workers fail to join unions the explanation sometimes advanced relates to the structural ambiguity of their position in the production process. For though, like the factory worker, they are hired labour, their tasks are oriented towards shareholder interests. What has been found more difficult to understand is why those in routine non-manual occupations have not joined unions *en masse*, since today the character of their employment is virtually indistinguishable from that of manual workers. To claim, as Gagliani has done, that if it were not for the fact that so many women are employed in these jobs, then income levels would still be clearly superior to those available to manual workers, is to miss the point: the fact is that income levels are low.[23] And to suggest that these women's working conditions are superior to those in all manual occupations is untenable, as McNally's descriptions of clerical working conditions clearly reveal.[24] It is very difficult, then, to label these occupations as 'middle class'. Others have tried to dismiss the question by appealing to women's lack of independence as political animals and irrelevance to the class structure (see chapter 15). There is clearly a need for research here; but there is every reason to suppose that the low level of unionisation amongst women clerical workers has to do with the qualities of their work environment, and their not unjustified perception of the trade union movement as having little time for women workers, and as subscribing to the view of women's employment as subsidiary.

CLASS CONSCIOUSNESS AND REVOLUTION

Social inequality has not noticeably declined, if the evidence is taken to be reliable; so what processes and mechanisms are succeeding in maintaining the present social and economic system? In other words, why is there no revolution in sight?

A traditional response points to the 'safety-valve' effect of social mobility in providing a basis for the perception of equality of opportunity, regardless of the reality. It also has the useful side-effect of 'creaming off' potential revolutionary working class leaders into high-status occupations—i.e. buying them off. Structural change in the economy has allowed for an excess of upward over downward mobility since the Second World War, which may well have accentuated this safety-valve function. Redistribution and social welfare measures have further helped to promote stability by blunting the sharpest edges of social inequality.

From a different standpoint, Banks has identified the institutionalisation of working-class protest as instrumental in the transformation of confrontation into compromise and adjustment.[25] Trade unions' early demands have been met; trade union leaders have lost much of their former radicalism as they have been incorporated more and more into industrial and governmental decision-making processes. They no longer belong to the ruled, but to the rulers. The increasing scale and bureaucratisation of trade union structure has inevitably led to a lack of real contact between the leadership and the rank and file (although this does vary considerably).

Giddens is of the opinion that recognition of the possibility of overall reorganisation of society by class action (i.e. revolutionary class consciousness) is not attainable unless people can distance themselves from the 'here and now'—in other words, are able to conceive of different patternings of social reality on an abstract level. This he sees as not possible for those who have been in a similar situation for generations.[26] He seems to suggest that a sudden, dramatic disjunction is needed before people can utilise their visionary potential. The scale of the shock required could be likened to what would happen if all factory workers were to wake up tomorrow and find they had been replaced by robots during the night. Implicit in Giddens's hypothesis, then, is that revolutions occur only when the pace of social change suddenly, unexpectedly, and sharply increases in a manner which is threatening to a large number of people. Such a proposition is difficult to refute: it can always be argued that change has not yet reached that critical point.

Others see the potential for revolutionary change as decidedly on the upswing, especially since advanced western societies may well be approaching the limits to growth. For Goldthorpe, this potential arises from a mature and established working class facing a weak and divided middle class—the suggested consequence of patterns of social mobility today.[27] For Westergaard, this potential is encapsulated in continued social inequality together with a growing working-class resentment that the trade unions and, in Britain, the Labour Party, have not lived up to their promises.[28]

But are there many today who are prepared to exert themselves for political change of any kind? There is evidence from both sides of the Atlantic that political alienation has grown considerably: voting participation has declined and support for the established parties has waned. People see little opportunity for influencing events. Where large numbers of the population have disengaged themselves from political activity or interest, there is no possibility for any popular change. A tendency to 'turn inwards' has been noted by numerous social observers in both Europe and North America in the 1970s. It can be argued, though, that this reaction to political discontent can only survive as long as the affluent lifestyle to which westerners have become accustomed is maintained. This can no longer be guaranteed: Europeans and North Americans have had to accept a modest decline in their living standards towards the end of the 1970s, and there is every sign that this trend will continue through the 1980s. Thus, it may not be coincidental that the turn of the decade has seen a rejuvenation of grassroots-based political initiatives, founded in large measure upon a concern for the environment, the threats posed to world peace, and the plight of the Third World. In the United States this has been manifested by a mushrooming of social movements and pressure groups, now spreading to Europe. In Britain, a new party (the SDP) has been formed almost overnight; in West Germany, the environmentally (and 'alternative lifestyle') focused 'Greens' have secured increasing support from the electorate. There is little here that is obviously revolutionary, but that such developments have emerged at all does indicate a possible return to the conviction that social and political change *can* be achieved by collective efforts.

Postscript on state socialist societies

It seems desirable to add a postscript—and it can be little more than that—on structured social inequality in European societies variously described as state socialist or communist. Though the circumstances surrounding the birth of these societies have not conformed to the Marxian pattern of a bourgeoisie being overthrown by a working class conscious of having been exploited and of its power to remedy the situation, private ownership of the means of production no longer exists. This of itself, together with the other major changes introduced, might be expected to have created entirely new stratification patterns or even to have eliminated social inequality altogether. We may look first at similarities which some observers have claimed to see between these patterns in Soviet-type and Western capitalist economies, and then at differences.

SIMILARITIES

One form of alleged similarity which was said to be manifesting itself, related to the imperative whereby developments in technology imposed on all advanced industrial societies, regardless of their political systems, a more and more standard type of stratification scheme in occupational and related terms. We have already had occasion to notice that available empirical data did not support this so-called convergence theory as it applied to the case of Britain and the United States. But there seems still to be some supporting evidence for this thesis as applied to the present case.

A rather different type of convergence between Western and Soviet-type societies was suggested by Geiger, to the effect that the increasing dominance of the state over the economy had created a situation in which, in both types of society, a ruling group had a controlling position in deciding the way in which the economic resources of the society should in fact be used and developed.[1]

A particularly interesting discovery of similarities between official Soviet ideology and the American Creed was made by Ossowski, a Polish sociologist, in the mid-1950s.[2] In both cases, he pointed out, there was a firm refusal to accept that in their type of society classes existed. Both, however, recognised that major inequalities, for example, in incomes, were to be found, and approval was accorded to these inequalities on the ground that they represented legitimate and necessary rewards for merit. When Turner put forward his suggested contrast between the ideologies underpinning the educational systems of England and the United States and, as we have seen, designated them as those of sponsored and contest mobility respectively, it was clear that the sponsored mobility model had equal applicability to Soviet-type societies. In their case, also, those who reached high positions in the most important spheres of life had been at all stages in their upward progress sponsored, and found suitable for continued support, by judges in membership of the ruling group.

A somewhat unexpected similarity came to light when Nowak conducted a survey in Poland in the early 1960s in which, among other things, respondents were asked to evaluate their position in society, as they saw it, compared with that of other people in that country.[3] Taking the two lowest points on the seven-point scale with which they were provided, as many as half the unskilled, and a third of the skilled, manual workers put themselves in the 'low' and the 'very low' categories, whereas very much smaller proportions of non-manual workers, and of those who were described as members of the creative intelligentsia and free professions, did so. Although direct comparison with the reactions of their counterparts in Britain or the United States to similar questions is not, for a variety of reasons, appropriate, the wide differentials in self-rating do suggest that the contrast between the two types of society may not be as great as has sometimes been supposed. In this and other surveys, incidentally, it was found that a very high proportion of respondents said they would like to see economic inequality reduced to a minimum. We do not, of course, know how far these expressed views are merely reflecting a basically egalitarian official ideology, nor can we provide corresponding expressed attitudes amongst the citizens of Western-type societies.

DIFFERENCES

Despite these and other possible similarities, most emphasis has on the whole tended to be laid on respects in which societies of the two types appear to be significantly different. 'Appear to be' is important, since opinions are naturally sharply divided on whether or not we should accept the officially promulgated view on most aspects of the matter. Is collective ownership, for example, a mere sham as (among many others) Djilas, the exiled ex-Vice-President of Yugoslavia claims?[4]

Two differences, however, are so obvious and so crucial as hardly to be open to question. First, the power wielded by the political bureaucracy is clearly much more nearly absolute than that possessed by the ruling group or groups in Britain or the United States. To say this is not necessarily to accept that the contrast takes the form suggested by Aron: a unified elite in the former case, and a divided one in the latter.[5] Whether or not there is in our two societies anything that can usefully be called a ruling class, the constraints within which those in control of affairs economically and politically have to operate, are both much more important and more wide-ranging than events have hitherto shown to apply to their counterparts in Soviet-type societies.

Secondly, because in these societies virtually all major economic and related policies are centrally planned, there is a sense in which the social stratification byproducts have been brought about *deliberately* and have not arisen in the relatively unplanned manner characteristic of Britain and the United States. The reward structure of USSR may not be of exactly the shape that the original architects of that society would have wished; but at least any major departure from the early blueprints has been deliberately arranged or allowed, for reasons that seemed overriding at the time, rather than taking place largely without either the knowledge or consent of those technically in control of affairs.

What, then, are the essential differences between the social stratification patterns of societies of these two types? Parkin notes that in the early period of socialist reconstruction the preceding balance of class advantages was necessarily fundamentally altered by all that took place—the educational reforms, the expropriation of landed estates and industrial property, and the attempt to introduce an egalitarian reward structure.[6] In the subsequent process of settling down, sometimes including a period of apparently going into reverse, there emerged a new occupational reward hierarchy which was partly a reflection of relative expertise scarcity, as in capitalist societies, but partly a response to non-market criteria such as the heaviness of the work or planning priorities. In this hierarchy Parkin sees the white-collar intelligentsia as forming the apex, with the skilled manual workers next in order of status and rewards, followed by routine non-manual workers (demoted by comparison with their position in our type of society), and with unskilled manual workers at the bottom.

Several points of particular interest emerge from this analysis. First, the manual/non-manual cleavage is clearly a less important one than it is with us. Degree of technical skill or training, rather than the *nature* of the work being done, has become the crucial consideration. Secondly, the white-collar intelligentsia has increasingly begun to displace manual workers in the higher reaches of the Communist Party—a process of deproletarianisation of the party has been taking place. The position of this intelligentsia is, however, significantly different from that of its nearest capitalist counterpart, the bourgeoisie. Thus, it cannot bequeath property to children, though it is able to secure for them important educational advantages. There is also much more upward movement from below, and Parkin sees this as taking the form of 'large-scale movements across the entire range of the reward hierarchy, not merely the interchange of personnel at the class margins'.[7]

Despite the infiltration of the intelligentsia into the party machine, Parkin lays great stress on the basic cleavage that nevertheless exists between the bureaucrats on the one hand, and the intelligentsia on the other.[8] These two groups are different in social background and education (peasant stock and lack of secondary education as against urban middle-class stock and university education). They also differ in that whilst the skills of the bureaucrats are specific to the job they have to do in one particular society, those of the intelligentsia are marketable across national frontiers. Inevitably the intelligentsia contrast the high public esteem in which they are held and their less favourable situation than that of their opposite numbers in other countries, with their lack of political power. Potentially this situation seems to many observers to contain the seeds of a Marxian type of class struggle, though there are many important points of difference from those involved in the classic formulation. It may be noted that, on Parkin's analysis of the position, in Soviet-type societies there is elite differentiation of a marked kind (that is, between the bureaucrats and the intelligentsia), whereas in advanced capitalist societies he sees a unified elite. This is in striking contrast to the Aron view, quoted on p. 160, to the effect that the former kind of society was characterised by a unified elite and the latter by a divided one.

It seems to be generally agreed that, apart from the other differences already mentioned, Soviet-type societies tend to show much smaller degrees of income differences between families at different ends of the social scale than are found in capitalist societies. One recent study suggests that the really significant difference in the social stratification system in the USSR is the absence of a private propertied class of great wealth.[9] Despite persistent official claims that a state of classlessness has been achieved, the position nevertheless seems to be that classes exist in Soviet-type societies, though they are not the same classes as are found in Western countries, and the significance attaching to their situation relative to each other is also different. Lane considers the preservation of the nuclear family to be partly responsible for the circumstance that economic, power and status inequalities have not withered away to the extent that might have been hoped for and expected. For as long as socialisation still remains to an important extent partly a family task, attitudes and even capacities can be transmitted to the next generation, despite the fact that wealth no longer can be. He notes that differences in life styles are still very pronounced, and that the trend seems to be, if anything, towards increasing the relative advantages of the children of the intelligentsia in access to education.

References and further reading

FOREWORD

1. Among books of selected readings providing substantial coverage relating to the issues with which we propose to deal, four in particular may be mentioned:

R. Bendix and S. M. Lipset, eds., *Class, Status and Power*, 2nd edn, New York, Free Press, 1966.

A. Beteille, ed., *Social Inequalities*, Penguin, 1969.

Celia S. Heller, ed., *Structured Social Inequality*, Collier-Macmillan, 1969.

G. Salaman, ed., *Stratification and Social Class*, London, Open University, 1972.

CHAPTER 1. SLAVE, CASTE AND FEUDAL RELATIONSHIPS

1. See E. Williams, *Capitalism and Slavery*, Deutsch, 1964, and S. M. Elkins, *Slavery: a problem in American institutional and intellectual life*, Chicago University Press, 1964.
2. See T. H. Pear, *English Social Differences*, Allen & Unwin, 1955.
3. L. Dumont, *Homo Hierarchicus: the caste system and its implications* (Paris, Gallimard, 1966), English trans., Weidenfeld & Nicholson, 1970, pp. 106–7.
4. *Ibid.*, p. 216.
5. *Ibid.*, p. 66; a contrary view is taken by G. D. Berreman, 'Caste in India and the United States', *American Journal of Sociology*, vol. 66, 1960–61.

6. See M. Bloch, *Feudal Society*, Routledge, 1962.

Further reading

F. K. Bailey, 'Closed social stratification', *European Journal of Sociology*, vol. 4, 1963.

B. Barber and E. G. Barber, eds., *European Social Class: stability and change*, New York, Macmillan, 1965.

E. R. Leach, ed., *Aspects of Caste in South India, Ceylon and Northwest Pakistan*, Cambridge University Press, 1960.

M. N. Srinivas, *Social Change in Modern India*, University of California Press, 1969.

CHAPTER 2. INTRODUCTION TO PART TWO

1. L. Dumont, *Homo Hierarchicus*, English trans., p. 11.

CHAPTER 3. DIFFERING THEORETICAL ORIENTATIONS

1. See T. B. Bottomore and M. Rubel, eds., *Karl Marx: Selected Writings*, Penguin, 1963.
2. See M. Weber, *Theory of Social and Economic Organisation*, New York, Free Press, 1964, and H. Gerth and C. Wright Mills, *From Max Weber*, 1961, and A. Sahay, ed., *Max Weber and Modern Sociology*, Routledge, 1971. A useful analysis and comparison of Marx and Weber on class and status is provided in J. Rex, *Key Problems of Sociological Theory*, Routledge, 1951, and also in A. Giddens, *Capitalism and Modern Social Theory*, Cambridge University Press, 1971.
3. See S. E. Finer, ed., *Pareto: Sociological Writings*, Pall Mall Press, 1966. One of the best short discussions of the principal elitist theories is to be found in T. B. Bottomore, *Elites and Society*, Penguin, 1966.
4. K. Davis and W. E. Moore, *American Sociological Review*, vol. 10, 1945.
5. D. Wrong, 'The functional theory of stratification: some neglected considerations', *American Sociological Review*, vol. 24, 1959.

6. M. M. Tumin, 'Some principles of stratification: a critical analysis', *American Sociological Review*, vol. 18, 1953.
7. G. A. Huaco, 'A logical analysis of the Davis-Moore theory of stratification', *American Sociological Review*, vol. 28, 1963.
8. K. Prandy, *Professional Employees: a study of scientists and engineers*, Faber, 1965.

Further reading

F. Parkin, ed., *The Social Analysis of Class Structure*, Tavistock, 1974.

A. Giddens, *Capitalism and Modern Social Theory*, Cambridge University Press, 1971.

A. Giddens, *The Class Structure of The Advanced Societies*, Hutchinson, 1973.

For aspects of Marxism, see R. Blackburn, ed., *Ideology in Social Science*, Fontana/Collins, 1972, Part III and 'Further reading'.

CHAPTER 4. ECONOMIC INEQUALITY

1. *Social Trends No. 12*, HMSO, 1982, Table 5.26.
2. Indirect taxes are those imposed on goods and services, paid only when these are bought, such as VAT or sales tax. These taxes are regressive (in contrast to income tax, which is progressive) because they fall more heavily on the less affluent in proportion to absolute income.
3. I. Robertson, *Social Problems*, New York, Random House, 1980, 2nd edn, pp. 196–8.
4. *Social Trends No. 12, op. cit.*, Ch. 5.
5. J. Westergaard and H. Resler, *Class in a Capitalist Society: a study of contemporary Britain*, Penguin, 1975, ch. 2.
6. US Bureau of the Census, *Statistical Abstract*, Washington, DC, Government Printing Office, 1978.
7. Derived from *Social Trends No. 12, op. cit.*, Table 5.17.
8. Derived from I. Reid, *Social Class Differences in Britain*, Open Books, 1981, 2nd edn, Table 3.11.
9. *Social Indicators 1973*, Washington, DC, 1973, Government

Printing Office, Chart 5/15; J. Hey, *Britain in Context*, Blackwell, 1979, p. 142. The most recent UK figures indicate that the top 25 per cent owned 82 per cent of the wealth (not including pension rights) in 1979, representing a decline of 4 per cent since 1971. *Social Trends, No. 12, op. cit.*, Table 5.26.

10. A minority group is any group of people who because of their physical or cultural characteristics are singled out from the others in the society in which they live for differential and unequal treatment. See H. M. Hacker, 'Women as a minority group', *Social Forces*, vol. 30, Oct. 1951, pp. 60–9, reprinted in J. Freeman, ed., *Women: A feminist perspective*, Palo Alto, Calif., Mayfield, 1979, 2nd edn. pp. 505–20.
11. See, for example, R. D. Barron and G. M. Norris, 'Sexual divisions and the dual labour market', ch. 3 in D. L. Barker and S. Allen, eds., *Dependence and Exploitation in Work and Marriage*, Longman, 1976.
12. A. Giddens, *The Class Structure of the Advanced Societies*, Hutchinson, 1973, pp. 218–20.
13. G. Lenski, *Power and Privilege: a theory of social stratification*, New York, McGraw-Hill, 1966.
14. H. S. Becker *et al.*, *Boys in White: student culture in a medical school*, University of Chicago Press, 1961.
15. H. D. Dickinson, *Institutional Revenue*, Williams and Norgate, 1932.
16. R. Collins, 'Functional and conflict theories of educational stratification', *American Sociological Review*, vol. 36, 1971.
17. Robertson, *op. cit.*, p. 325.
18. W. G. Runciman, *Relative Deprivation and Social Justice*, Routledge, 1966.
19. See F. Hirsch and J. H. Goldthorpe, eds., *The Political economy of Inflation*, Martin Robertson, 1978.
20. *Social Trends, No. 12, op. cit.*
21. T. Noble, *Structure and Change in Modern Britain*, Batsford, 1981, p. 288.

22. To determine where elite membership ends and that of the topmost social group begins is a matter of some moment, for it affects calculation of mobility rates in and out of the elite. For a discussion, see A. Giddens, 'Elites in the British Class Structure', ch. 1 in P. Stanworth and A. Giddens, eds., *Elites and Power in British Society*, Cambridge University Press, 1974.
23. Evidence abounds. See for Britain: Stanworth and Giddens, *op. cit.*; J. Urry and J. Wakeford, eds., *Power in Britain*, Heinemann, 1973. For the United States: R. A. Rothman, *Inequality and Stratification in the United States*, Englewood Cliffs, NJ, Prentice-Hall, 1978.
24. Though not all. See R. E. Pahl and J. T. Winkler, 'The economic elite: theory and practice', ch. 6 in Stanworth and Giddens, *op. cit.*
25. P. Stanworth and A. Giddens, 'An economic elite: a demographic profile of company chairmen', ch. 5 in Stanworth and Giddens, *op. cit.*
26. Giddens (1973), *op. cit.*, ch. 9.
27. M. Useem and A. McCormack, 'The dominant segment of the British business elite', *Sociology*, vol. 15, no. 3, Aug. 1981.
28. Giddens, *ibid.*
29. Comment made at the SSRC Conference on Occupational Mobility, University of Aberdeen, 1975.

Further reading

S. M. Miller and P. Robey, *The Future of Inequality*, New York, Basic Books, 1970.

A. B. Atkinson and A. J. Harrison, *The Distribution of Personal Wealth in Britain*, Cambridge University Press, 1978.

C. D. Harbury and D. M. Hitchens, *Inheritance and Wealth Inequality in Britain*, Allen and Unwin, 1979.

P. Townsend, *Poverty in the United Kingdom*, Penguin, 1979.

Material resulting from the Royal Commission on the Distribution of Income and Wealth, under the chairmanship of Lord Diamond, includes no fewer than eight major reports, the earliest published in July 1975 and the last in October 1979.

Those content with a 30-page summary of the findings, illustrated by excellent charts and diagrams, should consult *An A-Z of Income and Wealth: an everyman's guide*, HMSO, 1980.

CHAPTER 5. POWER INEQUALITY IN COMMUNITY AND SOCIETY

1. This point is made by D. C. Miller, 'Decision-making cliques in community power structures', *American Journal of Sociology*, vol. 64, 1958.
2. From the very large number of reports on these investigations, the following can be singled out:
   United States: R. Dahl, *Who Governs? Democracy and Power in an American City*, Yale University Press, 1961.
   P. H. Rossi, 'Power and community structures', in L. A. Coser, ed., *Political Sociology*, Harper & Row, 1966.
   R. A. Schermerhorn, *Society and Power*, Random House, 1961.
   W. Spinard, 'Power in local communities', in J. L. Price, ed., *Social Facts*, Collier-Macmillan, 1969.
   Britain: A. H. Birch, *Small Town Politics* (Glossop), Oxford University Press, 1959.
   I. Emmett, *A North Wales Village*, Routledge, 1964.
   R. Frankenberg, *Communities in Britain*, Penguin, 1966.
   J. Littlejohn, *Westrigg: the Sociology of a Cheviot Parish*, Routledge, 1963.
   Margaret Stacey, *Tradition and Change: A Study of Banbury*, Oxford University Press, 1960.
   W. M. Williams, *The Sociology of an English Village* (*Gosforth*), Routledge, 1956.
3. C. Wright Mills, *The Power Elite*, Oxford University Press, 1959.
4. D. Riesman, *The Lonely Crowd*, Yale University Press, 1950.
5. *Ibid.*, p. 244.
6. Hugh Thomas, ed., *The Establishment*, London, Anthony Blond, 1959.
7. Hugh Thomas, ed., *Crisis in the Civil Service*, London, Anthony Blond, 1968, p. 7.

Further reading
See chapter 6 below.

CHAPTER 6. POWER INEQUALITY WITHIN SECTORS AND OCCUPATIONS

1. S. Keller, *Beyond the Ruling Class*, Random House, 1963.
2. A much fuller account of the position will be found in R. K. Kelsall, *Higher Civil Servants in Britain*, Routledge, 1955.
3. See, e.g. D. H. J. Morgan, 'The social and educational background of Anglican bishops', *British Journal of Sociology*, vol. 20, 1969, and C. B. Otley, 'The educational background of British Army Officers', *Sociology*, vol. 7, 1973.

   A specialised aspect of the breadth or narrowness of the social band from which members of an *occupation* are drawn relates to the extent of 'following in father's footsteps' in the sense of a son or daughter actually being engaged in the same field of work as father previously was. How much 'occupational self-recruitment' there was (a narrower concept than that of 'status-category self-recruitment' to be discussed in chapter 14 below) at different times, has been estimated for various occupations in Britain—medicine, the law, the Church, school-teaching, the higher civil service—and major differences in this respect have been found. See for example R. K. Kelsall, 'Self-recruitment in four professions', chapter XI in D. V. Glass, ed., *Social Mobility in Britain*, Routledge, 1954.
4. See W. L. Guttsman, *The British Political Elite*, MacGibbon and Kee, 1968, and R. Johnson, 'The British political elite, 1955–72', *European Journal of Sociology*, 1973.

Further reading for chapters 5 and 6

On the issues discussed in chapters 5 and 6, see particularly:

P. Stanworth and A. Giddens, eds., *Elites and Power in British Society*, Cambridge University Press, 1974.

J. Urry and J. Wakeford, eds., *Power in Britain*, Heinemann, 1973.

R. Dahrendorf, *Class and Class Conflict in Industrial Society*, Routledge, 1959.

CHAPTER 7. STATUS INEQUALITY

1. E. Shils, 'Deference' in J. A. Jackson, ed., *Social Stratification*, Cambridge University Press, 1968.
2. For Lloyd Warner see notes 3–5 below. Reference has already been made to some English local community studies in chapter 5. A useful discussion of the extent of their comparability will be found in A. Weinberg and F. Lyons, 'Class theory and practice', *British Journal of Sociology*, vol. 32, 1972.
3. W. Lloyd Warner and P. S. Lunt, *The Social Life of a Modern Community*, Yale University Press, 1941, p. 81.
4. W. Lloyd Warner, *Democracy in Jonesville*, New York, Harper, 1949, p. xv.
5. W. Lloyd Warner, M. Meeker and K. Eells, *Social Class in America*, Chicago, Harper & Row, 1949.
6. K. Mayer, 'The theory of social classes', *Transactions of the Second World Congress of Sociology*, vol. 2 (1954), p. 327.
7. P. K. Hatt, C. C. North *et al.*, *Occupations and Social Status*, New York, Free Press, 1961.
8. R. W. Hodge, P. M. Siegel and P. H. Rossi, 'Occupational prestige in the United States 1925–63', *American Journal of Sociology*, vol. 70, 1964.
9. This emerged from the North/Hatt enquiry, when respondents were asked the basis on which they concluded that a job had excellent standing; the other factor of roughly equal importance to pay and education was the degree to which the job was essential and served humanity.

CHAPTER 8. HOW MANY DIMENSIONS AND HOW ARE THEY INTERRELATED?

1. This is more usually called *status* consistency, but that

usage conflicts with our concept of status. Other terms used include 'status crystallisation' and 'status congruity'.
2. G. E. Lenski, *Power and Privilege*, McGraw-Hill, 1966.
3. W. G. Runciman, 'Class, status and power' in J. A. Jackson, ed., *Social Stratification*, Cambridge University Press, 1968, p. 30.
4. G. K. Ingham, 'Social stratification: individual attributes and social relationships', *Sociology*, vol. 4, 1970, pp. 105–113.
5. F. Parkin, *Class Inequality and Political Order*, MacGibbon & Kee, 1971.
6. *Ibid.*, p. 46.

CHAPTER 9. INEQUALITY OF LIFE EXPECTANCY

1. The issues discussed in this paragraph are also dealt with in R. K. Kelsall, *Population*, 4th edn, Longman, 1979.
2. Those interested in the complications of marrying working-age mortality data with social class groupings should consult A. J. Fox and P. O. Goldblatt, *Longitudinal Study: socio-demographic mortality differentials*, HMSO, 1982. This is a first report on mortality in 1971–75 based on a one per cent sample of the usually resident population of England and Wales derived from the 1971 Census.
3. J. W. B. Douglas and J. M. Blomfield, *Children Under Five*, Allen & Unwin, 1958. See also *Perinatal and Infant Mortality: social and biological factors 1975–77* (Studies on Medical and Population Subjects No. 41), HMSO, 1980–81.
4. 'The main findings of the comparative study of social and biological effects on perinatal mortality', *World Health Statistics Report*, vol 31, no. 1, 1978.
The full report of the study is in several volumes, *Social and Biological Effects on Perinatal Mortality*, Budapest, Statistical Publishing House, 1978.
5. *Population Trends* 9, HMSO, Autumn 1977, p. 13.

CHAPTER 10. INEQUALITY OF ACCESS TO EDUCATIONAL AND CAREER OPPORTUNITIES

1. R. K. Kelsall and H. M. Kelsall, *Social Disadvantage and Educational Opportunity*, Holt, Rinehart & Winston, 1971.
2. A. Little and J. Westergaard, 'The trend of class differentials in educational opportunity in England and Wales', *British Journal of Sociology*, vol. 15, 1964.
3. R. K. Kelsall, A. Poole and A. Kuhn, *Six Years After*, Higher Education Resarch Unit, Sheffield University, 1970; and *Graduates: the sociology of an elite*, Methuen, 1972.

Further reading

M. Carter, *Into Work*, Penguin, 1966.

M. Craft, ed., *Family, Class and Education*, Longman, 1970.

C. Jencks, *Inequality: a reassessment of the effects of family and schooling in America*, Allen Lane/Penguin, 1973.

G. Taylor and N. Ayres, *Born and Bred Unequal*, Longman, 1969.

P. Wedge and H. Prosser, *Born to Fail?*, Arrow Books for National Children's Bureau, 1973.

A. H. Halsey, A. F. Heath and J. M. Ridge, *Origins and Destinations: Family, Class and Education in Modern Britain*, Oxford, Clarendon Press, 1980.

D. Spender and E. Sarah, eds., *Learning to Lose: Sexism and Education*, The Women's Press, 1980.

CHAPTER 11. INEQUALITY OF ACCESS TO HOUSING

1. J. Rex and R. Moore, *Race, Community and Conflict*, Routledge, 1967.
2. R. E. Park, E. W. Burgess and R. D. McKenzie, *The City*, University of Chicago Press, 1925.
3. E. Gittus, 'Sociological aspects of urban decay' in F. Medhurst and J. Parry Lewis, eds., *Urban Decay*, Macmillan, 1969, p. 28.
4. A. S. Barnett, C. G. Pickvance and R. H. Ward, 'Some factors underlying racial discrimination in housing: a preliminary report on Manchester', *Race*, vol. 12, 1970.

5. J. G. Davis and J. Taylor, 'Race, community and no conflict', *New Society*, 9 July, 1970.
6. W. G. Runciman, 'Race and social stratification', *Race*, vol. 13, 1973, p. 507.
7. *Ibid.*, p. 506.

CHAPTER 12. CLASS-RELATED ATTITUDES AND BEHAVIOURS

1. For fuller discussion of these issues see R. K. Kelsall and H. M. Kelsall, *Social Disadvantage and Educational Opportunity*, Holt, Rinehart & Winston, 1971.
2. M. Goldberg, 'Factors affecting educational attainment in depressed urban areas', in *Education in Depressed Areas*, Teachers College Press, Columbia University, 1963, p. 87.
3. See R. K. Kelsall and H. M. Kelsall, *op. cit.*
4. R. C. Rist, 'Student social class and teacher expectations: the self-fulfilling prophecy in ghetto education', *Harvard Educational Review*, vol. 40, 1970.
5. *Ibid.*, p. 191.
6. R. McKenzie and A. Silver, *Angels in Marble*, Heinemann, 1968; see also E. Nordlinger, *The Working Class Tories*, MacGibbon & Kee, 1967.
7. S. Steinberg and G. J. Selznick, 'Social class, ideology and voting preference', reprinted in C. S. Heller, *Structured Social Inequality*, Collier-Macmillan, 1969.
8. B. Sarlvik and I. Crewe, Decade of Re-alignment, Cambridge University Press, 1983.

Further reading

See chapter 13 below.

CHAPTER 13. DIFFERING CONSTRUCTIONS OF REALITY

1. This is, of course, an inadequate summary of the theory propounded in P. L. Berger and T. Luckmann, *The Social Construction of Reality*, Allen Lane, 1967.

2. P. Hiller, 'Social reality and social stratification', *Sociological Review*, vol. 21 (1973), 93.
3. D. Lockwood, 'Sources of variation in working-class images of society', *Sociological Review*, vol. 14, 1966.
4. F. Parkin, *Class, Inequality and Political Order*, MacGibbon & Kee, 1971.
5. Prandy, as we saw in an earlier chapter, provided empirical evidence on this, in his study of a particular segment of British society.
6. R. Centers, *The Psychology of Social Class*, Princeton University Press, 1949.
7. N. Gross, 'Social class identification in the urban community', *American Sociological Review*, vol. 18, 1953.
8. W. G. Runciman, *Relative Deprivation and Social Justice*, Routledge, 1966, p. 207.

Further reading for chapters 12 and 13

J. Bonham, *The Middle Class Vote*, Faber, 1954.
J. Klein, *Samples from English Cultures*, 2 vols., Routledge, 1967. ledge, 1967.
C. A. Valentine, *Culture and Poverty*, University of Chicago Press, 1968.
K. Roberts *et al.*, *The Fragmentary Class Structure*, Heinemann, 1977.
M. Bulmer, ed., *Working Class Images of Society*, Routledge, 1975.
M. Stacey *et al.*, *Power, Persistence and Change*, Routledge, 1975.
K. Roberts, *The Working Class*, Longman, 1978.
J. Raynor, *The Middle Class*, Longman, 1969.
R. King and N. Nugent, eds., *Respectable Rebels*, Hodder & Stoughton, 1979.

CHAPTER 14. SOCIAL MOBILITY

1. S. M. Lipset and R. Bendix, *Social Mobility in Industrial Society*, University of California Press, 1959.
2. J. Westergaard and H. Resler, *Class in a Capitalist Society: a*

study of contemporary Britain, Harmondsworth, Penguin, 1975, Part IV.

3. *Ibid.*
4. For example, Kingsley Amis recounts the adventures of *Lucky Jim*, a working-class boy who becomes a university lecturer and sets out to scandalise those in authority. Another instance is John Braine's *Room at the Top*.
5. F Musgrove, *The Migratory Elite*, Heinemann, 1963.
6. B. Jackson and D. Marsden, *Education and the Working Class*, Penguin, 1966 (Revised edition).
7. T. Noble, 'In pursuit of pure mobility', *Sociology*, vol. 13, 1979.
8. It is widely recognised that occupation alone cannot capture the full depth of the concept of social mobility; the trend in the United States to describe such research as the study of *occupational* mobility is an honest admission of this.
9. T. Noble, *op. cit.*
10. A. I. Harris and R. Clausen, *Labour Mobility in Great Britain, 1953–63* Government Social Survey for the Ministry of Labour, London, HMSO, 1967.
11. L. A. Chisholm, 'The comparative career development of graduate women and men' *Women's Studies International Qtly* vol. 1, 1978. For a fuller discussion of women and social stratification, see chapter 15.
12. J. H. Goldthorpe, C. Llewellyn and C. Payne, *Social Mobility and Class Structure in Modern Britain*, Oxford, Clarendon Press, 1980.
13. D. V. Glass, ed., *Social Mobility in Britain*, Routledge, 1954.
14. For a description and comparison of social class and occupational prestige scales, see I. Reid, *Social Class Differences in Britain*, Open Books, 1981, 2nd edn, ch. 2. For a full account of the methodology of the 1972 Nuffield social mobility survey, see Goldthorpe, Llewellyn and Payne, *op. cit.* Briefly, the Nuffield study ranked respondents with reference to two kinds of ratings:

(i) The *market* (source and size of income, job security,

opportunity for upward mobility) and *work* (social relationships at the workplace) situations of the respondent.

(ii) Allocation to one of seven social classes as follows:

Class I: higher-grade professionals, administrators, managers and large proprietors;

Class II: lower-grade professionals, etc., higher-grade technicians, supervisors of non-manual workers;

Class III: routine non-manual and sales personnel;

Class IV: farmers, small proprietors, the self-employed (except professional);

Class V: supervisors of manual workers, lower-grade technicians;

Class VI: skilled manual workers;

Class VII: semi-skilled and unskilled manual workers, agricultural labourers.

15. A. Heath, *Social Mobility,* Fontana/Collins, 1981, ch. 2.
16. J. H. Goldthorpe, C. Payne and C. Llewellyn, 'Trends in class mobility', *Sociology*, vol. 12, 1978.
17. J. H. Goldthorpe and C. Llewellyn, 'Class mobility in modern Britain', *Sociology*, vol. 11, 1977.
18. J. Banks, *Prosperity and Parenthood*, Routledge, 1954.
19. See R. K. Kelsall, *Population*, 4th edn, Longman, 1979.
20. D. Pearce and M. Britton, 'The decline in births: some socio-economic aspects', *Population Trends* 7, Spring 1977.
21. D. F. Swift, 'Social class and achievement motivation', in D. F. Swift, ed., *Basic Readings in the Sociology of Education*, London, Routledge, 1970; p. 197.
22. L. Reissman, *Inequality in American Society: Social Stratification*, Glenview, Ill., Scott, Foresman, 1973; D. W. Rossides, *The American Class System*, Boston, Houghton Mifflin, 1967; R. M. Hauser *et al.*, 'Temporal change in occupational mobility: evidence for males in the United States', *American Sociological Review*, vol. 40, 1975.
23. R. H. Turner, 'Modes of social ascent through education: sponsored and contest mobility' in A. H. Halsey, J. Floud

and C. A. Anderson, eds., *Education, Economy and Society*, New York, Free Press of Glencoe, 1961.

24. A. C. Kerckhoff, 'Stratification Processes and Outcomes in England and the US', *American Sociological Review*, vol. 39, 1974.
25. S. Lieberson and D. K. Carter, 'Making it in America', *American Sociological Review*, vol. 44, 1979.
26. Heath, *op. cit.*, p. 77.
27. *ibid.*, ch. 3.
28. *ibid.*, ch. 5.
29. A. H. Halsey, A. F. Heath and J. M. Ridge, *Origins and Destinations: Family, Class and Education in Modern Britain*, Oxford, Clarendon Press, 1980. For a short and simply written summary of the findings, see A. H. Halsey, 'Social Mobility and Education', ch. 14 in D. Rubinstein, ed., *Education and Equality*, London, Harper & Row, 1979.
30. This term, which has quickly gained acceptance in sociological discourse, is attributed to Bourdieu (see: P. Bourdieu, 'Cultural reproduction and social reproduction', in R. Brown, ed., *Knowledge, Education and Cultural Change*, Tavistock, 1973; P. Bourdieu and J-C. Passeron, *Reproduction in Education, Society and Culture*, Sage, 1977). It refers to the knowledge, skills and social connections with which privileged parents can endow their offspring and thus transmit high social status indirectly. Richardson, for a London sample investigated in the early 1970s, located the reasons for the downward mobility of the skilled manual sons of non-manual fathers importantly in a *lack* of access to cultural capital, arising from the 'peripheral' middle class status of the family of origin: one or both parents had been upwardly mobile from the working class. Such downward mobility, Richardson argues, is really only status consolidation, since the sons are returning to the 'real' status position of their parents. (C. J. Richardson, 'The problem of downward mobility',

British Journal of Sociology, vol. 28, 1977). This position has not gone uncriticised: see R. Bland, 'The operational definition of downward mobility', *British Journal of Sociology*, vol. 29, 1978 (Richardson's reply can be found in the same issue, pp. 374–5), and T. Noble, *Structure and Change in Modern Britain*, Batsford, 1981, pp. 214–16.

CHAPTER 15. SEXUAL STRATIFICATION AND SOCIAL STRATIFICATION

1. N. Claude-Mathieu, *Ignored by some, denied by others: the social sex category in sociology* (Explorations in Feminism No. 2), Women's Research and Resources Centre Publications, 1977.
2. F. Parkin, *Class Inequality and Political Order*, MacGibbon & Kee, 1971.
3. A. Giddens, *The Class Structure of the Advanced Societies*, Hutchinson, 1973.
4. J. Westergaard and H. Resler, *Class in a Capitalist Society: a study of contemporary Britain*, Harmondsworth, Penguin, 1975, ch. 6.
5. J. H. Goldthorpe, C. Llewellyn and C. Payne, *Social Mobility and Class Structure in Modern Britain*, Oxford; Clarendon Press, 1980.
6. H. H. Davis, *Beyond Class Images: Explorations in the Structure of Class Consciousness*, Croom Helm, 1979.
7. Incisive critiques of this practice can be found in: M. Porter, 'Worlds apart: the class consciousness of working class women', *Women's Studies International Qtly*, vol. 1, 1978; M. Goot and E. Reid, *Women and Voting Studies: Mindless Matrons or Sexist Scientism?* (Sage Professional Papers), Sage, 1975; C. F. Epstein, 'Women and Power: the roles of women in politics in the United States', ch. 8 in C. F. Epstein and R. L. Coser, *Access to Power: Cross-National Studies of Women and Elites*, London, Allen & Unwin, 1981.

8. A. Heath, *Social Mobility*, Glasgow, Fontana/Collins, 1981, ch. 4.
9. J. Acker, 'Women and social stratification: a case of intellectual sexism', *American Journal of Sociology*, vol. 78, 1972–3.
10. P. Rossi *et al.*, 'Measuring household social standing', *Social Science Research*, vol. 3, 1974.
11. *Higher Education* (The Robbins Report) Command 2154 HMSO, 1963; A. C. Kerckhoff, 'Marriage and occupational attainment in Great Britain and the United States', *Journal of Marriage and the Family*, vol. 40, 1978.
12. See I. Reid, *Social Class Differences in Britain*, Open Books, 1981, Tables 3.17A and B; *Social Trends No. 6*, HMSO, 1975, Table 1.1.
13. E. Garnsey, 'Women's work and theories of class stratification', *Sociology*, vol. 12, 1978.
14. A. Schlegel, 'Toward a theory of sexual stratification', ch. 1 in A. Schlegel, ed., *Sexual Stratification: a cross-cultural view*, Columbia University Press, 1977.
15. Acker, *op. cit.*
16. See Garnsey, *op. cit.*, and J. West, 'Women, sex and class', ch. 9 in A. Kuhn and A-M. Wolpe, eds., *Feminism and Materialism: women and modes of production*, London, Routledge, 1978.
17. L. Comer, 'The question of women and class', *Women's Studies International Qtly*, vol. 1, 1978.
18. The wealth of material poses problems of bibliographic selection. As introductory overviews, see for Britain: E. Byrne, *Women and Education*, Tavistock, 1978; L. Mackie and P. Pattullo, *Women at Work*, Tavistock, 1977. For the United States: N. Frazier and M. Sadker, *Sexism in School and Society*, New York, Harper & Row, 1973; C. F. Epstein, *Women's Place: options and limits on professional careers*, University of California Press, 1970; J. Freeman, ed., *Women: a feminist perspective*, California, Mayfield, 1979, especially Parts 3 and 4.
19. Heath, *op. cit.*, ch. 4.

20. Acker, *op. cit.*
21. Heath, *ibid.*
22. L. A. Chisholm, 'The comparative career development of graduate women and men', *Women's Studies International Qtly*, vol. 1, 1978.
23. Heath, *ibid.*
24. J. C. Goyder and P. C. Pineo, 'Female occupational achievement', Paper presented to the Annual Meeting of the Canadian Sociology and Anthropology Association, Kingston, Ontario, 1973.
25. Chisholm, *op. cit.*
26. L. Marsden, E. Harvey and I. Charner, 'Female graduates: their occupational mobility and attainments', *Canadian Review of Sociology and Anthropology,* vol. 12, 1975.
27. P. England, 'Women and occupational prestige: a case of vacuous sex equality', *Signs*, vol. 5, 1979.
28. H. Etzkowitz, 'The male Sister: sexual separation of labour in society', *Journal of Marriage and the Family*, vol. 33, 1971.
29. W. M. Sewell, R. M. Hauser and W. C. Wolf, 'Sex, schooling and occupational status', *American Journal of Sociology*, vol. 86, 1980; L. A. Chisholm and D. Woodward, 'The experiences of women graduates in the labour market', ch. 12 in R. Deem, ed., *Schooling for Women's Work*, Routledge, 1980.
30. C. F. Epstein, 'Women and elites: a cross-national perspective', ch. 1 in Epstein and Coser, *op. cit.*
31. Epstein, ch. 9 *op. cit.*, in Epstein and Coser, *ibid.*; C. F. Epstein, 'Encountering the male establishment: sex-status limits on women's careers in the professions', *American Journal of Sociology*, vol. 75, 1970.
32. R. L. Coser, 'Where have all the women gone? Like the sediment of a good wine, they have sunk to the bottom', ch. 2 in Epstein and Coser, *op. cit.*
33. J. E. Prather, 'When the girls move in: a sociological analysis of the feminisation of the bank teller's job', *J. of Marriage and the Family*, vol. 33, 1971.

34. R. Crompton, 'Trade unionism and the insurance clerk', *Sociology*, vol. 13, 1979.

CHAPTER 16. THEMES OF CURRENT DEBATE

1. J. A. Kahl, 'Some social concomitants of industrialisation and urbanisation', ch. 1 in W. A. Faunce, ed., *Readings in Industrial Sociology*, Englewood Cliffs, N.J., Prentice-Hall, 1967; C. Kerr *et al.*, 'Industrialism and world society', ch. 1 in J. M. Shepard, ed., *Organisational Issues in Industrial Society*, Englewood Cliffs, N.J., Prentice Hall, 1972.
2. J. H. Goldthorpe, 'Social stratification in industrial society', in P. Halmos, ed., *Sociological Review Monograph No. 8*, 1964.
3. E. Garnsey, 'Occupational structure in industrialised societies: some notes on the convergence thesis in the light of Soviet experience', *Sociology*, vol 9, 1975.
4. P. M. Blau and O. T. Duncan, *The American Occupational Structure*, New York, John Wiley, 1967.
5. A. Heath, *Social Mobility*, Glasgow, Fontana/Collins, 1981, ch. 6.
6. S. M. Lipset and R. Bendix, *Social Mobility in Industrial Society*, University of California Press, 1959; S. M. Miller, 'Comparative and social mobility', *Current Sociology*, vol. 9, 1960.
7. Heath, *op. cit.*, ch. 7.
8. D. H. Wrong, 'Social inequality without social stratification', in C. S. Heller, ed., *Structured Social Inequality*, Collier-Macmillan, 1969.
9. A. Marwick, *Class: Image and Reality in Britain, France and the USA since 1930*, Glasgow, Collins, 1980 (Fontana, 1981), Introduction.
10. R. P. Coleman and L. Rainwater, *Social Standing in America: New Dimensions of Class*, New York, Basic Books, 1978.
11. Marwick, *op. cit.*, ch. 15.

12. A. Giddens, *The Class Structure of the Advanced Societies*, Hutchinson, 1973, ch. 6.
13. T. B. Bottomore, *Classes in Modern Society*, Allen & Unwin, 1965.
14. See, for example, R. King, 'The middle class in revolt?', ch. 1 in R. King and N. Nugent, eds., *Respectable Rebels: middle class campaigns in Britain in the seventies,* Hodder & Stoughton, 1979.
15. T. Noble, *Structure and Change in Modern Britain*, Batsford, 1981, ch. 8.
16. J. Westergaard, 'Sociology: the myth of classlessness', in R. Blackburn, ed., *Ideology in Social Science*, Glasgow, Fontana/Collins, 1972.
17. Giddens, *op. cit.*
18. Is Giddens himself confusing indispensability with power here? At a different point in his analysis he accuses others of precisely this error, using Weber's famous analogy to demonstrate his argument: if indispensability necessarily confers power, then in a slave economy the slaves would be dominant (Giddens, *op. cit.*, p. 173).
19. J. H. Goldthorpe, D. Lockwood, F. Bechhofer and J. Platt, *The Affluent Worker*, 3 vols, Cambridge University Press, 1968–9.
20. J. Westergaard, 'The rediscovery of the cash-nexus', in R. Miliband and J. Saville, eds., *The Socialist Register 1970*, Merlin, 1970.
21. R. L. Davis and J. Cousins, 'The "new working class" and the old', ch. 11 in M. Bulmer, ed., *Working-class Images of Society*, London, Routledge, 1975.
22. T. May, 'Middle class unionism', ch. 5 in King and Nugent, *op. cit.*
23. G. Gagliani, 'How many working classes?', *American Journal of Sociology*, vol. 87, 1981.
24. F. McNally, *Women for Hire: a study of the female office worker*, Macmillan, 1979.
25. J. Banks, *Marxist Sociology in Action*, Faber, 1970.

26. Giddens, *op. cit.*, ch. 6.
27. J. H. Goldthorpe and C. Llewellyn, 'Class mobility in Britain: three theses examined', *Sociology*, vol. 11, 1977.
28. J. Westergaard (1972), *op. cit.*

POSTSCRIPT ON STATE SOCIALIST SOCIETIES

1. T. Geiger, 'Class society in the melting pot', in C. S. Heller, ed., *Structured Social Inequality*, Collier-Macmillan, 1969.
2. S. Ossowski, *Class Structure in the Social Consciousness*, Routledge, 1963.
3. S. Nowak, 'Changes of social structure in social consciousness', in C. S. Heller, ed., *op. cit.*
4. M. Djilas, *The New Class*, Thames & Hudson, 1957.
5. R. Aron, 'Social structure and the ruling class', *British Journal of Sociology*, vol. 1, 1950.
6. F. Parkin, *Class, Inequality and Political Order*, MacGibbon & Kee, 1971.
7. *Ibid.*, p. 157.
8. F. Parkin, 'System contradiction and political transformation', *European Journal of Sociology*, 1972.
9. D. Lane, *The End of Inequality? Stratification under state socialism*, Penguin, 1971.

Further reading

C. E. Black, ed., *The transformation of Russian Society*, Harvard University Press, 1960.
M. Bornstein and D. R. Fusfeld, eds., *The Soviet Economy*, Irwin, Homeland, 1970.
P. Hollander, ed., *American and Soviet Society*, Prentice-Hall, 1969.
A. Inkeles, *Social Change in Soviet Russia*, Harvard University Press, 1968.
A. Inkeles and K. Geiger, eds., *Soviet Society*, Constable, 1961.
A. Kassof, ed., *Prospects for Soviet Society*, Pall Mall Press, 1968.
F. Parkin, 'Class stratification in socialist societies', *British Journal of Sociology*, vol. 20, 1969.

N. Wesolowski and K. Slomczynski, 'Social stratification in Polish cities', in J. A. Jackson, ed., *Social Stratification*, Cambridge University Press, 1968.

Author Index

Acker, J. 180, 181
Allen, S. 167
Amis, K. 176
Anderson, C. A. 178
Aron, R. 160, 162, 184
Atkinson, A. B. 168
Aryes, N. 173

Bailey, F. K. 165
Banks, J. A. 127, 177, 184
Barber, B. 165
Barber, E. G. 90, 165
Barker, D. L. 167
Barnett, A. S. 173
Barron, R. D. 167
Bechhofer, F. 183
Becker, H. S. 32, 167
Bendix, R. 103, 114, 164, 176, 182
Berger, P. L. 175
Bernstein, B. 133
Berreman, G. D. 164
Beteille, A. 41, 164
Birch, A. H. 169
Black, C. E. 184
Blackburn, R. 166
Bland, R. 179
Blau, P. M. 10, 148, 182
Bloch, M. 165
Blomfield, J. M. 172
Bonham, J. 175
Bornstein, M. 21, 184
Bottomore, T. B. 89, 150, 165, 183
Bourdieu, P. 178
Braine, J. 176
Britton, M. 177
Brown, R. 178
Bulmer, M. 175, 183
Burgess, E. W. 173
Byrne, E. 180

Carter, D. K. 130, 178
Carter, M. 111, 173
Centers, R. 175
Charner, I. 181
Chisholm, L. A. 176, 181
Claude-Mathieu, N. 179
Clausen, R. 121, 122, 176
Coleman, R. P. 183
Collins, R. 33, 167
Comer, L. 180
Coser, L. A. 169
Coser, R. L. 180, 181, 182
Cousins, J. 183
Craft, M. 173
Crewe, I. 174
Crompton, R. 182

Cutright, P. 41

Dahl, R. 169
Dahrendorf, R. 25, 171
Davidson, N. 81
Davis, H. H. 179
Davis, J. G. 93, 174
Davis, K. 23, 165
Davis, R. L. 183
Deem, R. 181
Dickinson, H. D. 33, 167
Djilas, M. 160, 184
Douglas, J. W. B. 172
Dumont, L. 8, 9, 15, 164, 165
Duncan, O. 148, 182

Eells, K. 64, 171
Elkins, S. M. 3, 164
Emmett, I. 41, 169
Engels, F. 113
England, P. 181
Epstein, C. F. 180, 181, 182
Etzkowitz, H. 181

Faunce, W. A. 182
Finer, S. E. 21, 165
Floud, J. 178
Fox, A. J. 172
Frankenberg, R. 41, 169
Frazier, N. 180
Freeman, J. 167, 181
Fusfeld, D. R. 184

Gagliani, G. 154, 184
Garnsey, E. 147, 180, 182
Geiger, T. 159, 184, 185
Gerth, H. 18, 165
Giddens, A. N. 18, 29, 38, 39, 135, 150, 151, 156, 165, 166, 167, 168, 170, 179, 183, 184
Gittus, E. 90, 173
Glass, D. V. 112, 123, 125, 126, 170, 176
Goldberg, M. 95, 174
Goldblatt, P. O. 172
Goldthorpe, J. H. 36, 100, 122, 125, 131, 136, 146, 147, 156, 167, 176, 177, 179, 182, 183, 184
Goot, M. 179
Goyder, J. C. 181
Gross, N. 111, 175
Gularnick, L. 78
Guttsman, W. L. 59, 170

Hacker, H. M. 167
Halmos, P. 182
Halsey, A. H. 132, 173, 178
Harbury, C. D. 168
Harris, A. I. 121, 122, 176
Harrison, A. J. 168
Harvey, E. 181
Hatt, P. K. 64, 171
Hauser, R. M. 178, 181
Heath, A. F. 125, 126, 131, 132, 136, 173, 177, 178, 180, 181, 182
Heller, C. S. 164, 174, 182, 184
Hey, J. 167
Hiller, P. 107, 175
Hirsch, F. 167
Hitchens, D. M. 168
Hodge, R. W. 65, 171
Hollander, P. 184
Huaco, G. A. 23, 166

Ingham, G. K. 73, 172
Inkeles, A. 185

Jackson, B. 118, 176

Jackson, J. A. 171, 172, 185
Jencks, C. 173
Johnson, R. 59, 170

Kahl, J. A. 182
Kassof, A. 185
Keller, S. 49, 170
Kelsall, H. M. 82, 95, 173, 174
Kelsall, R. K. 52, 82, 87, 95, 170, 172, 173, 174, 177
Kerckhoff, A. C. 130, 178, 180
Kerr, C. 182
King, R. 175, 183
Klein, J. 175
Kuhn, A. 86, 173, 180

Lane, D. 162, 184
Leach, E. R. 165
Lenski, G. 30, 72, 167, 172
Lieberson, S. 130, 178
Lipset, S. M. 114, 164, 175, 182
Little, A. 86, 173
Littlejohn, J. 41, 169
Llewellyn, C. 122, 176, 177, 179, 184
Lloyd Warner, W. 62, 63, 64, 67, 68, 171
Lockwood, D. 108, 109, 175, 183
Luckmann, T. 103, 175
Lunt, P. S. 62, 171
Lyons, F. 62, 171

McCormack, A. 39, 168
McKenzie, R. D. 89, 99, 100, 173, 174
Mackie, L. 180
McNally, F. 155, 184
Marsden, D. 118, 176
Marsden, L. 181
Marwick, A. 150, 183
Marx, K. 18, 19, 20, 21, 24, 25, 40, 42, 45, 47, 57, 62, 65, 66, 71, 91, 92, 109, 113, 116, 135, 149, 150, 151, 158, 166
May, T. 183
Mayer, K. B. 64, 171
Meeker, M. 64, 171
Miliband, R. 183
Miller, D. C. 41, 169
Miller, S. M. 167, 168, 182
Moore, R. 89, 90, 91, 92, 93, 165, 173
Moore, W. E. 23, 165
Morgan, D. H. J. 54, 170
Musgrove, F. 117, 128, 176

Noble, T. 36, 121, 150, 167, 176, 179, 183
Nordlinger, E. 174
Norris, G. M. 167
North, C. C. 64, 171
Nowak, S. 159, 184
Nugent, N. 175, 183

Ossowski, S. 159, 184
Otley, C. B. 54, 170

Pahl, R. E. 168
Pareto, V. 21, 22, 42, 115
Park, R. E. 89, 173
Parkin, F. 73, 74, 75, 109, 135, 139, 161, 162, 166, 172, 175, 179, 184, 185
Passeron, J-C. 178
Pattullo, P. 180
Payne, C. 176, 177, 179
Pear, T. H. 6, 164

Pearce, D. 177
Pickvance, C. G. 90, 173
Pineo, P. C. 181
Platt, J. 183
Poole, A. 86, 173
Porter, M. 179
Prandy, K. 24, 110, 166, 175
Prather, J. E. 182
Price, J. L. 169
Prosser, H. 173

Rainwater, L. 183
Raynor, J. 175
Reid, E. 179
Reid, I. 166, 176, 177, 180
Reissman, I. 177
Resler, H. 116, 135, 138, 166, 176, 179
Rex, J. 18, 89, 90, 91, 92, 93, 165, 173
Richardson, C. J. 178, 179
Ridge, J. M. 132, 173, 178
Riesman, D. 42, 169
Rist, R. C. 97, 98, 174
Roberts, K. 175
Robertson, I. 166, 167
Robey, P. 168
Rossi, P. 41, 65, 169, 171, 180
Rossides, D. W. 177, 178
Rothman, R. A. 168
Rubel, M. 18, 165
Rubinstein, D. 178
Runciman, W. G. 34, 73, 93, 111, 112, 167, 172, 174, 175

Sadker, M. 181
Sahay, A. 18, 165
Salaman, G. 164
Sarah, E. 173
Sarlvik, B. 174
Saville, J. 183
Schermerhorn, R. A. 41, 169
Schlegel, A. 180
Selznick, G. J. 101, 174
Sewell, W. M. 181
Shepard, J. M. 182
Shils, E. 61, 171
Siegel, P. M. 65, 171
Silver, A. 99, 100, 174
Slomczynski, K. 185
Spender, D. 173
Spinard, W. 41, 169
Srinivas, M. N. 165
Stacey, M. 41, 169, 175
Stanworth, P. S. 38, 168, 170
Steinberg, S. 101, 174
Swift, D. F. 128, 177

Taylor, G. 173
Taylor, J. 93, 174
Thomas, H. 44, 169
Townsend, P. 81, 168
Tumin, M. M. 23, 166
Turner, R. H. 129, 130, 159, 178

Urry, J. 168, 170
Useem, M. 39, 168

Valentine, C. A. 175
Veblen, T. 68

Wakeford, J. 168, 170
Ward, R. H. 90, 173
Weber, M. 16, 18, 20, 21, 25, 40, 62, 72, 91, 151, 165
Wedge, P. 173
Weinberg, A. 62, 171

Wesolowski, W. 185
West, J. 180
Westergaard, J. H. 116, 135, 138, 150, 152, 156, 166, 173, 176, 179, 183, 184
Williams, E. 3, 164
Williams, W. M. 41, 169
Winkler, J. T. 168
Wolf, W. C. 181
Wolpe, A-M. 180
Woodward, D. 181
Wright Mills, C. 18, 42, 44, 165, 169
Wrong, D. H. 23, 149, 165, 182

Subject Index

'affluent worker', 100, 151–3

class, *see* inequality
class concept, usefulness of, 63, 73–5, 91–2, 148–51, 163
class conflict/war, 19, 21, 42, 47, 89, 92, 155–7
class consciousness/ideology, 19, 21, 36, 42, 47, 136, 150, 155–7
class-related attitudes, behaviours, 55, 94–102
class theory, 18–21
constructions of reality, differing, 103–13
conveyance or divergence? 146–8

elite(s)
  circulation of, 21–2
  differentiation, 39, 162
  economic, 36–40, 43–4, 58–9, 130–1
  governing, 21–2
  migratory, 118
  occupational, 49–58, 130–2, 143–4
  political, 43–4, 48, 59–60, 144
  power, 42–8
  strategic, 43, 48, 49–58
  unified, 160, 162
embourgeoisement, 151–3
ethnicity, 3–4, 29, 69–70, 75, 89–93, 130–1

'feminisation' of an occupation, 144–5
fertility, 127–8
functionalist approach, 22–3, 31–3

inequality
  avowed
    caste relationships, 5–10
    feudal relationships, 10–12
    slave relationships, 3–5
  career success/prospects, 87–8, 131–2, 140–5
  career aspirations, 115
  dimensions
    number and interrelations, 20, 62, 71–5
    rank-order consistency, 72, 171–2
  economic, ix, 7–8, 25–40, 72–5, 104–18
    causes, 30–1
    extent of, 25–8

in income, 27–8
in wealth, 28–9
occupational differences in, 31–3
progress in reducing, 29–30
social consequences, 33–5
educational access, 30, 82–7, 132–3
fertility, 127–8
health, 76–81
housing access, 89–93
life chances, 57, 82–8
life expectancy, 76–81
power
in local communities, 7–8, 41–2
in sectors and occupations, 49–60
in society, 42–8
sexual, 28, 134–45
conventional approaches, 137–8
redifinition of issues, 138–40
theory and research, 134–7
what do we know? 140–5
status, 5–9, 20–1, 61–70, 72–5
community, 62–4
occupational, 64–7, 140–5
inflation, 35–6

'managerial revolution', 37–9
manual/non-manual distinction, 19, 27–8, 66–7, 111–12, 125, 161
'meaning systems', 109
mortality
general, 76–9
infant, 79–80

non-elite, 21–2, 42

political party allegiance, 98–102, 136
proletarianisation, 153–5

'relative deprivation', 34, 111–12
revolution, why none? 155–7

self-rating, 111–12
self-recruitment
occupational, 170
status-category, 123–7
sexual stratification, 134–45
social mobility
'contest and sponsored', 129–30, 159
effects on individuals and families, 117–19
individual factors influencing upward, 128–9
industrial societies compared, 129–30, 148
intergenerational, 114, 121–3
methodological difficulties, 119–21
routes to upward, 117, 131–2
societal implications, 114–16
women's, 140–5
state socialist societies, 158–63
status, *see* inequality
stratification, *see* inequality

theoretical orientations, differing, 18–24

'underclass', 29, 150
voting behaviour, 98–102